AF621765

THE JOURNEY TO ASSOCIATE DIRECTOR AND CHOREOGRAPHER . . . AND BEYOND

*"**THE JOURNEY TO ASSOCIATE DIRECTOR AND CHOREOGRAPHER . . . AND BEYOND** is the book I wish I had when I was dreaming of doing just that. A must-read necessary tool for anyone considering being on the 'other side of the table.' Richard J. Hinds puts into one book many of the answers it took me seventeen years as an associate and assistant to discover. Can't wait for the second edition because the only thing constant on Broadway is change! And we are all the better for it"!*

Jerry Mitchell, Tony Award-winning Director and Choreographer

*"**THE JOURNEY TO ASSOCIATE DIRECTOR AND CHOREOGRAPHER . . . AND BEYOND** tells the truth about what it means to be an associate: the responsibility, the humility, the trust, and the deep care required to hold a show and support a vision that isn't yet your own. Richard J. Hinds writes from real experience, with clarity and generosity, and without pretense. As someone who has relied on exceptional associates throughout my career, I believe deeply in mentorship and in passing knowledge forward. This book does exactly that. It offers guidance, encouragement, and a clear sense of what excellence looks like in the room—not just artistically, but humanely. If you are committed to collaboration, integrity, and growth, this book will feel like someone finally put your experience—and your aspirations—into words."*

Sergio Trujillo, Tony Award-winning Director and Choreographer

"Few people bring the extraordinary blend of experience, artistry, and heart quite like Richard J. Hinds. With a track record of being trusted on major projects—the kind with big budgets, firm deadlines, and the occasional backstage crisis—and a vibrant voice as both director and choreographer, Richard offers guidance that's equal parts practical and inspiring, like advice that lands right on the beat with a crisp snap of a fan! Anyone who's had the absolute joy of working with Richard—as I have—will recognize that same unmistakable spirit leaping straight off these pages."

Marcia Milgrom Dodge, Tony Award-nominated Director and Choreographer

*"If there is any chance that you might be interested in pursuing a career as an Associate Director or Choreographer, **THE JOURNEY TO ASSOCIATE DIRECTOR AND CHOREOGRAPHER . . . AND BEYOND** is essential reading."*

Jeff Calhoun, Tony Award-nominated Director and Choreographer

"Richard J. Hinds offers a comprehensive first-hand account of the complexities and artistry of associate work. His advice is truly full of wisdom. His knowledge and how clearly he lays out the work, is beautifully articulated. I personally believe a path from working as an associate to then choreographer or director offers such a fertile learning ground for understanding how to build a musical or play."

Lorin Latarro, Tony Award-nominated Director and Choreographer

"This book is INCREDIBLE . . . I so wished I had someone like Richard J. Hinds guiding me twenty years ago. This book is a beautiful guide to taking control of your future, how you show up every day, building relationships, trusting yourself, knowing you are prepared but equally flexible. Richard, you are giving the industry, and a new generation, a true gift, thank you."

Sarah Ogleby, Broadway Choreographer

"This book brilliantly articulates what makes an associate indispensable. Clear, generous, and deeply practical—a must-read for anyone supporting a director or choreographer."

Lisa Stevens, Director and Choreographer

THE JOURNEY TO ASSOCIATE DIRECTOR AND CHOREOGRAPHER . . . AND BEYOND

An Industry Guide for Practitioners and Creatives

RICHARD J. HINDS

methuen | drama
LONDON • NEW YORK • OXFORD • NEW DELHI • SYDNEY

METHUEN DRAMA
Bloomsbury Publishing Plc, 50 Bedford Square, London, WC1B 3DP, UK
Bloomsbury Publishing Inc, 1359 Broadway, New York, NY 10018, USA
Bloomsbury Publishing Ireland, 29 Earlsfort Terrace, Dublin 2, D02 AY28, Ireland

BLOOMSBURY, METHUEN DRAMA and the Methuen Drama logo are trademarks of Bloomsbury Publishing Plc

First published in Great Britain 2026

Copyright © Richard J. Hinds, 2026

Richard J. Hinds has asserted his right under the Copyright, Designs and Patents Act, 1988, to be identified as author of this work.

For legal purposes the Acknowledgements on p. xi constitute an extension of this copyright page.

Cover design by Jade Barnett
Cover images by Richard J. Hinds
Paper texture by Josua Brieden / Unsplash

All rights reserved. No part of this publication may be: i) reproduced or transmitted in any form, electronic or mechanical, including photocopying, recording or by means of any information storage or retrieval system without prior permission in writing from the publishers; or ii) used or reproduced in any way for the training, development or operation of artificial intelligence (AI) technologies, including generative AI technologies. The rights holders expressly reserve this publication from the text and data mining exception as per Article 4(3) of the Digital Single Market Directive (EU) 2019/790.

Bloomsbury Publishing Plc does not have any control over, or responsibility for, any third-party websites referred to or in this book. All internet addresses given in this book were correct at the time of going to press. The author and publisher regret any inconvenience caused if addresses have changed or sites have ceased to exist, but can accept no responsibility for any such changes.

No rights in incidental music or songs contained in the work are hereby granted and performance rights for any performance/presentation whatsoever must be obtained from the respective copyright owners.

A catalogue record for this book is available from the British Library.

A catalog record for this book is available from the Library of Congress.

ISBN: HB: 978-1-3505-7880-7
PB: 978-1-3505-7879-1
ePDF: 978-1-3505-7881-4
eBook: 978-1-3505-7882-1

Typeset by RefineCatch Limited, Bungay, Suffolk
Printed and bound in Great Britain

For product safety related questions contact productsafety@bloomsbury.com.

To find out more about our authors and books visit www.bloomsbury.com
and sign up for our newsletters.

CONTENTS

LIST OF FIGURES

FOREWORD

If there is any chance that you might be interested in pursuing a career as an Associate Director or Choreographer, *The Journey to Associate Director and Choreographer . . . and Beyond* is essential reading.

Bob Fosse, Michael Bennett, Gower Champion, Susan Stroman, Casey Nicholaw, Jerry Mitchell, Tommy Tune—every great theatre director and choreographer has relied heavily on their associates. As collaborative an art form as theatre is, there is no more important relationship than that between a director or choreographer and their associate. Associates must not only understand the artistic vision but also safeguard it—often long after that vision has faded from memory.

Before beginning my own career as a director and choreographer, I was fortunate to serve as an associate to nine-time Tony Award–winning director/choreographer Tommy Tune. It was during that time that I learned just how much responsibility an associate carries; think of it as a theatrical marriage. Later, when it came time for me to choose my own associates, I became exceptionally discerning. From personal experience, I can say without hesitation that Richard J. Hinds is among the very best.

When Richard asked me to write this foreword, I was surprised to discover that a book like this had never been written. Although it is true that there is no substitute for learning on the job, the comprehensive knowledge Richard has gathered—and the clarity with which he presents it—offers an education comparable to a Rhodes Scholar's training in the world of theatre.

I can honestly say that *Newsies* would not have become the success it was without my—and Christopher Gattelli's—extraordinary associates, Richard J. Hinds and Lou Castro. This book prepares its readers not just to survive the responsibilities of a great associate, but to excel in the trenches of the theatrical landscape.

Jeff Calhoun, Tony Award-nominated Director and Choreographer

Jeff Calhoun and Richard J. Hinds in rehearsals for *Jekyll & Hyde*.

Credit: Billy Bustamante

ACKNOWLEDGEMENTS

There are so many people to thank for helping me arrive at this moment, and I am deeply grateful to each and every one of you who has played a role in this journey.

I would like to begin by acknowledging the associates who have made it their mission to support directors and choreographers. Your dedication, generosity, and passion are the backbone of so much of what we do, and it does not go unnoticed. I am especially grateful to those who generously shared their experiences and advice in this book: Ashley Andrews, Ashley Rodbro, Cedric Dodd, Conner Wilson, Danny Sharron, DB Bonds, Kasey RT Graham, Lauren Stroud, Lizz Picini, Lou Castro, Rachelle Rak, Rickey Tripp, Sarah Parker, Tavia Rivée Jefferson, Travis Waldschmidt, and Voltaire Wade-Green.

I would also like to recognize the incredible creatives I have had the privilege of serving as an assistant and associate to. Your artistry, leadership, and trust have shaped me in ways I will carry with me forever: Alex Timbers, Andy Blankenbuehler, Annie-B Parson, Bill Fennelly, Brian Burke, Ellenore Scott, Jeff Calhoun, Kelly Devine, Liam Steel, Lisa Stevens, and Tye Blue.

To the many associates who have stood by my side throughout my career—you continually challenge, inspire, and elevate me, and I am better because of you: Aimee Lane, Alec Mann, Andrew Turteltaub, Anthony Raimondi, Brandon Kelly, Elyn Collier, Frankie Paparone, Holly Prentice, Jane Bunting, Jennifer Jancuska, Josh Zacher, Lauren Stroud, Lizz Picini, Marjorie Failoni, Matthew Whennell-Clark, Morgan Rose, Patrick Garr, Phil Colgan, Renée Albulario, Ruby McMann, Sam Hooper, and Trent Soyster.

Thank you to the many individuals who contributed to the making of this book. Your time, insight, and support helped bring this project to life: Adam Wachter, Dom O'Hanlon, Felix Dunning, Helen Siveter, Jeff Whiting, Jill Gold, Marcia Milgrom Dodge, Mark Jones, Melinda Atwood, Phil Gleaden, Randy Adams at SDC, and Rosie Colosi.

To my aunt and uncle, Angela D'Valda Sirico and Steve Sirico—thank you for introducing me to the world of dance and theatre and for supporting me from the very first moment I stepped into your studio. You helped spark something in me that would grow into a lifelong passion.

To the rest of my family, thank you for your unwavering love and encouragement. You have always believed in me, even in moments when I doubted myself.

To my partner in crime, Matthew Whennell-Clark—who has read every page of this book more times than I can count—thank you. Your constant support, patience, and belief in me mean more than words can fully express. Thank you, sweetie!

To my sister, Jessica, who has endured countless dance competitions, puppet shows, and years of me singing showtunes at the top of my lungs—thank you for always cheering me on. Your love and support have never gone unnoticed.

And finally, but certainly not least, my mom, Lori. I would not be where I am today without your unconditional love and support. You have been my foundation, my champion, and my greatest source of strength. You helped turn my dreams into reality and gave me the confidence to dream big and reach for the stars.

Richard J. Hinds with Jessica Bujdud (sister) and Lori Hinds (mother).
Credit: Richard J. Hinds

INTRODUCTION

My Journey

Throughout my time as an associate, most of what I learned was from "on-the-job" experiences, as there was no official "how-to" guide. Knowing that there are minimal resources to help associates learn the tricks of the trade, I was inspired to write this book, a comprehensive resource designed to share my insights and those of many other associates. I hope this book offers you a clearer understanding of the expectations of this role and provides you with practical guidance should you then want to transition into the role of director or choreographer.

My career has spanned over theatre, television, and film offering me the opportunity to hone my craft as an associate on some of the industry's most celebrated productions. I've served as an associate on six Broadway shows—*Elf, Company, Come From Away, Newsies, Jekyll & Hyde*, and *Il Divo: A Musical Affair*, as well as the North American and UK tours of *Come From Away, Elf, 9 to 5,* and Disney's *High School Musical*. My associate career extended to London's West End on productions of *Titanique*, *Elf*, *Come From Away*, and *Here Lies Love* at the National Theatre. I have worked at numerous regional theatres in America including Paper Mill Playhouse, La Jolla Playhouse, The Old Globe, Deaf West, Kansas City Repertory Theatre, The 5th Avenue Theatre, Seattle Rep, and Ford's Theatre, as well as iconic New York City venues including Radio City Music Hall, Jazz at Lincoln Center, and Hammerstein Ballroom.

Steve Sirico and Angela D'Valda Sirico.
Credit: Dash *at London's Domion Theatre*

I was born in Norwalk, CT and my training began under the guidance of my aunt and uncle, Angela D'Valda Sirico and Steve Sirico, who had achieved success as an adagio couple performing in *Dash,* a show conceived and directed by Wayne Sleep (principal dancer with The Royal Ballet and the original Mr. Mistoffelees in the West End production of *Cats*). After their extensive performing career around the world, they settled down to open "D'Valda and Sirico's Dance Fitness Connection" in Fairfield, CT. I began training at the studio from the age of four and quickly joined the competitive team in which professionalism and excellence were expected of me very early on. I was pushed and inspired on a day-to-day basis, especially with the impressive roster of fellow dancers who trained alongside me, including American Ballet Theatre's James B. Whiteside, Broadway choreographer Dominique Kelley (*The Great Gatsby*), and *The Voice* winner, Alisan Porter. From the first time I hit the stage at Showbiz National Dance Competition and had an audience in front of me who were cheering and clapping, I knew I was exactly where I was meant to be. The competition world was where many of my early professional relationships were first found.

Richard J. Hinds at the age of 9.
Credit: Angela D'Valda Sirico and Steve Sirico

Living only forty-five minutes away from New York City allowed frequent visits to the legendary Broadway Dance Center (BDC) where I studied under acclaimed teachers such as Frank Hatchett, Charles Kelley, and Michele Assaf, all pivotal leaders shaping the dance community of their era. The opportunity to train under such legends propelled my learning curve at an extraordinary pace. As these teachers recognized my connection to Angela and Steve, there was more attention thrown my way, resulting in me being pushed even harder. The faculty at BDC became more like mentors to me than just teachers. They recognized my passion for dance and did everything they could to support me. These many trips to New York City, dancing alongside working professionals, required that I learned how to be very focused and display a good work ethic from a young age. It became quickly evident that dance was much more than just a hobby; it was destined to be my career.

Richard J. Hinds at the age of 12.
Credit: Angela D'Valda Sirico and Steve Sirico

Although the constant support of my aunt and uncle was invaluable, it was my mother who truly shaped my life and career. She recognized very early that dance and theatre were my passion and she did whatever she could to support that. As a single mother dedicated to making ends meet for my sister Jessica and I, she worked multiple jobs to make sure that my love for dance and seeing Broadway shows was never pushed aside. The holiday season always brought with it a tradition that I waited for all year long. It would start by me creating a list of Broadway shows that I was interested in seeing, I'd present it to her, and she would go on to ultimately choose what shows we would attend. Then on a Friday in December, we'd make the journey from Connecticut to the Marriott Marquis Hotel right in the middle of Times Square. Our three-day stint would begin with a Friday evening performance, two shows on Saturday, and a final Sunday matinee performance before returning home absolutely buzzing, stocked full of merchandise and signed Playbills.

It was during one of those trips to New York City at the age of eight years old that my future became crystal clear. My mother and I arrived at the Winter Garden Theatre to see *Cats* not quite knowing exactly what to expect. Within moments of walking into the theatre, I was completely mesmerized. The way the set spilled into the audience was completely magical, blurring the lines between the stage and the audience. As the show began, the performers filed through the audience to make their way to the stage wearing the most incredible costumes and intricate makeup that completely transformed them. But more than anything, it was the dancing that truly captivated me. I had never seen anything like this theatrical spectacle before. As the show ended and the lights came up, I had made the decision that I wanted to be on Broadway, but more specifically in *Cats*!

Now being a complete *Cats* enthusiast, I began listening to the double cassette tape day in and day out. I was even inspired to create a puppet show of *Cats* in its entirety, all two hours and forty-five minutes including an intermission, using freshly picked pieces of garbage from the trash as scenery and several packages of paper lunch bags dressed with yarn to be the cats. Once my mother stopped yelling at me for stealing her Christmas lights and having garbage all over the basement, she enjoyed the show and clearly appreciated my creativity. My sister was less impressed.

As I approached my middle school years, I started looking for summer programs to continue challenging me as a dancer and to introduce me to more teachers and opportunities during the summer break. That moment arrived with a recommendation for the Interlochen Arts Camp, an eight-week summer program in Michigan that offered intensive training in a variety of art disciplines. It took some convincing but eventually my mother agreed to let me attend the summer following my eighth grade year at thirteen years old. The instant I stepped onto the campus, I knew I had arrived somewhere truly special, a place that would shape my future. I was immediately struck by the passion radiating from every student for their chosen art form and was overwhelmed by the amount of people my age who were just as eager to pursue a career in the arts as I was. I quickly went from being a big fish in a small pond to being a small fish in a big pond. It was very humbling. The male dancers around me were executing leaps and pirouettes far more advanced than I was able to, reinforcing just how much more training lay ahead for me. The program itself was demanding yet incredibly rewarding. Days were filled with hours of classes in different dance styles culminating in a performance at the end of the fourth and eighth week where we would showcase what we had learned. The summer flew by and upon returning to Connecticut, I immediately dove back into training and competitions with even more fire and passion. As soon as applications opened for the following summer, I pleaded with my mother yet again, and she agreed to let me return to Interlochen.

My second summer marked a turning point. Sharon Randolph, the head of the Academy's Dance Division, invited me to attend Interlochen Arts Academy (IAA), a year-round boarding school. Convincing my mother to let me attend the summer camp was one thing, but leaving for an entire school year would be another story. Through many conversations, supported by calls from the school administrators, her reservations eventually softened and she agreed. Upon returning home from camp, I had a couple of weeks to prepare before returning back to Michigan, this time with my mother by my side. Having never been, she wanted to see the campus firsthand, which was completely understandable since I would now be living there for the entire school year. Upon arrival, her skepticism quickly dissipated as she witnessed the very place that had captivated me. After a tearful farewell, she returned to Connecticut, and my dedicated training commenced.

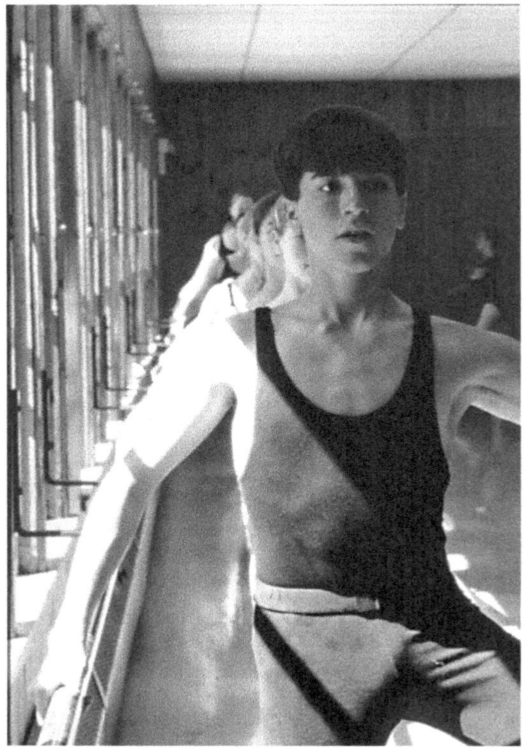

Richard J. Hinds at Interlochen Arts Camp.
Credit: © ARTICA - Archives of the Interlochen Center for the Arts

Life as a dance major demanded discipline as we were challenged both academically and artistically. IAA teaches a college-preparatory curriculum, which meant our classes were quite challenging. Although we were attending an arts school, our education was not to be compromised on any level. Our mornings were dedicated to academic coursework; once completed, we would head to lunch before continuing to the dance building, where we spent an average of four to six hours a day training—often longer on weekends. Afternoons typically began with intensive technique classes, focused primarily on the foundations of ballet and modern, before transitioning into rehearsals for upcoming performances. These ranged from full-length ballets, such as *The Nutcracker* and *Sleeping Beauty*, to choreography showcases and dance concerts.

The dance department, led by Sharon Randolph, Wendy Masterson, and Michael Tevlin, provided us with a wealth of knowledge and guidance. We were also fortunate to work with numerous guest artists who exposed us to a diverse range of dance styles and helped shape us into well-rounded performers. Among the many classes offered, it was the choreography classes that really captured my attention. For the first time, I was challenged to discover my own artistic voice—conceiving ideas, selecting music, and translating them into movement. I quickly discovered a passion I didn't know I had and began to flex my creative muscles.

About halfway through my sophomore year, I started to become incredibly intrigued in what was happening in the theatre building. Although the dance and theatre departments were quite segregated, I began developing a relationship with the theatre faculty and eventually convinced them to let me take introductory theatre classes that did not conflict with my dance requirements. My passion for theatre quickly became evident to both the theatre department faculty and my

Interlochen Dance Faculty: Wendy Masterson, Michael Tevlin, and Sharon Randolph.
Credit: © ARTICA - Archives of the Interlochen Center for the Arts

academic advisors, including Jennifer Wesling. I began choreographing numbers for campus events such as "Casino Night" and coffee houses, which ultimately led to the school granting me the opportunity to direct and choreograph a full-length musical theatre review. I held auditions and cast the show, picked the song list from a collection of well-known musicals, and worked closely with several other students to design the show from top to bottom. This first real experience as a creative allowed me to explore a side of theatre I knew little about, and I found it incredibly fulfilling.

During my junior year at Interlochen, I made the decision to audition for Broadway Theatre Project (BTP), a theatre intensive in Tampa, Florida, under the legendary leadership of Ann Reinking. My audition submission consisted of a recorded dance combination, a monologue, and a song. Although the dance was a no-brainer, the acting and singing were uncharted territory. Thankfully, the faculty at Interlochen provided their support and were incredibly helpful in assisting me prepare my VHS audition submission. Fingers crossed, I sent it off, and the day the acceptance letter arrived, it felt like a dream. That summer became an unforgettable "embarrassment of riches" as my teachers included Broadway titans such as Ann Reinking, Gwen Verdon, Gregory Hines, James Naughton, Richard Maltby Jr., and Jeff Calhoun, to name a few. I thought Interlochen's training was rigorous, but BTP operated on a whole different level. The faculty didn't treat us as students; they were preparing young professionals. Our schedule was jam-packed. We trained all day, running from one class to the next, grabbing a quick bite, and immediately heading into rehearsals during the evening. The intensive culminated in a showcase where we performed a range of songs and dances—not only for friends and family, but also for renowned casting agents, directors, and choreographers. I was cast in several numbers, including "Bye Bye Blackbird," staged by Gwen Verdon, and a pas de deux to "You Must Love Me," choreographed by Ann Reinking. The opportunity to work so closely with these two legends is something I will never forget. Following the program, several students went on to perform in productions such as *Chicago, Fosse*, and *42nd Street*. Working one-on-one with such an esteemed faculty was both a rare privilege and a profoundly formative experience.

Richard J. Hinds with Ann Reinking.
Credit: Richard J. Hinds

Richard J. Hinds with Gwen Verdon.
Credit: Richard J. Hinds

Senior year arrived quickly, prompting me to turn my focus toward the next steps—most notably, the college application process. I set my sights on several top-tier musical theatre programs and attended the National Unified Auditions, an event in Chicago where a collection of elite schools gathers, offering the unique opportunity to audition for multiple institutions in one location. The process began with researching, selecting, and applying to the programs I hoped to be considered for.

On arriving in Chicago, I was immediately struck by the precision of the operation—a well-oiled machine in every sense. The event took place in a hotel convention center, where each school occupied its own ballroom. One by one, I moved from room to room, presenting my song and monologue before quickly transitioning to the next. The cycle repeated itself throughout the day with little pause. The pace was relentless. Being ushered along in such a structured, almost impersonal process left little opportunity to truly connect with the schools or their faculty. What stood out most was that only one program incorporated a dance call. As a result, most of my auditions assessed only my singing and acting—areas that, at the time, were far less developed than my dance training. By the end of the day, I had been seen by all eight universities to which I had applied. With the final audition behind me, all that remained was to wait.

As dance majors at Interlochen, we were required to audition for visiting college recruiters representing their institutions' dance departments. Although pursuing dance in college wasn't the path I ultimately envisioned for myself, I approached each audition with focus and intention, recognizing every one as an opportunity to grow. In time, I began receiving acceptance letters from several dance programs, many accompanied by generous scholarships—reflecting the high demand for male dancers. These offers promised a secure and successful future in dance, yet they didn't align with where I truly saw myself . . .

theatre was my passion. I continued to wait for responses from the musical theatre programs I had auditioned for at the National Unified Auditions. After weeks of anticipation, the final decision arrived: *I HAD BEEN REJECTED FROM EVERY SINGLE MUSICAL THEATRE SCHOOL I AUDITIONED FOR!*

I was absolutely devastated. Although this should have prompted me to reassess my theatrical aspirations, it did quite the opposite. I knew with complete certainty that my place was in theatre and I needed to figure out how to make that happen. My mother struggled to understand my dismissal of the dance scholarships I had received, but this was not where my heart was. The challenge now was to discover what my path forward would be to continue taking steps to working on Broadway. First things first, I needed to move to New York City!

In order to persuade my mother to grant me permission to move to New York City at the young age of seventeen, I had to demonstrate that I could manage myself financially. I started looking for summer performance opportunities that would offer me a paycheck, which led me to audition for Canobie Lake Park in New Hampshire. I booked the gig and spent my summer dancing my heart out to top hits from the 1990s in "*Mega Mix Live*" and performed in a Country revue sporting a black, white, and red cow print costume while doing the two-step. Every dollar that I earned that summer was more than just savings; it proved to me and my mother that I was able to be independent and take care of myself.

When I finally made the big move to New York City, I arrived with a sense of comfort and familiarity, having spent so much of my childhood there. Knowing that I had a support group and people looking out for me reassured my mother, allowing her to sigh with relief. I hit the ground running, and my immediate priority was to get a job to pay the bills.

A good friend of mine worked at Bath & Body Works, so it only made sense that I should apply for a job there too. After a successful interview, I quickly joined the team. I soon learned that my manager was a lover of theatre, and when she discovered I could dance, she became my biggest fan. My job duties soon included tapping around the store entertaining customers while singing original lotion inspired jingles. When clocking in for my shift, nothing about it felt like work and the time would fly by. My manager was incredibly supportive of my performance career and was very accommodating, letting me take time off for last-minute callbacks without any consequences. I was truly fortunate to have secured this job, not only was I getting paid, but I got to sing and dance while doing so.

When not performing at Bath & Body Works, I could be found at Broadway Dance Center, taking as many classes as possible and building relationships with the newest faculty members. Simultaneously, I started private vocal and acting classes, honing these crucial skills that I desperately needed to improve on to be taken seriously as a musical theatre performer. As I stepped into the audition scene, it became immediately clear that the industry was not only highly competitive, but often cutthroat in ways I hadn't yet experienced. Starting out as a Non-Equity performer meant spending hours in crowded hallways, waiting for a chance to be seen. Once inside the audition room, sometimes I would be kept through multiple cuts and other times dismissed almost immediately. The constant highs and lows became grueling, both mentally and physically. Still, regardless of the outcome, I kept going. I was finally living in New York City, and I was determined to let nothing stand in my way as I pursued my dreams.

After three months of hustling in New York City, I booked the European premiere of *Sisi, das musical*, a musicalization of the story of Empress Elisabeth of Austria. The experience was a whirlwind. We rehearsed in Vienna for three weeks and then performed for one week over the Christmas holidays in Munich. I could tell you more, but it's a story so intriguing and whacky it would need its own book. I will, however, tell you this; the show was completely in German yet there was no one there to teach us German, all the posters advertised "featuring an Ensemble straight from Broadway," and none of us had ever done a Broadway show, and last, but certainly not least, a horse showed up backstage on opening night and was put into the show thirty minutes before the curtain went up.

I booked my next professional job just weeks later, thanks to my teacher and mentor, Jill Gorrie. Once again, I returned to Europe to join the touring production of *Grease das Musical*, performing in the ensemble and understudying Eugene. The show had a high-energy, MTV-inspired style, with choreography by Melissa Williams and Carla Kama. It pushed my dance technique to its limits while giving me the opportunity to grow as an actor covering a principal role.

Upon returning to the United States, I booked the national tour of *Fosse*, where I was reunited with several faculty members I had previously worked with at Broadway Theatre Project. My track included performing "Spirit of Fosse" and "Steam Heat." We were especially fortunate to have Ann Reinking in the rehearsal room on multiple occasions, giving us the rare opportunity to learn the Fosse style directly from the legend herself.

After a year on the road, I got the opportunity to audition for the national tour of *Cats*. It was quite an intense process with multiple callbacks, allowing the team to make sure all the potential candidates could handle the demands of the material. Once the audition process was complete, the most grueling part of any casting process began . . . the waiting! A few weeks later while at the airport in Salt Lake City, Utah, returning home from a teaching gig, I was waiting for my flight when I received a call from Rachel Hoffman at Dave Clemmons Casting. I BOOKED *CATS*! The realization that I would be involved in the show that ignited my passion for musical theatre all those years ago felt like a dream come true. I was offered the role of dance captain and swing, covering six tracks. With this being my first time as a dance captain, I was now working in a position of management, which gave me the insight of how a production runs and what it takes to keep the machine going. Little did I know at the time that this knowledge would prove incredibly beneficial later in my career as an associate.

After completing my time with *Cats*, I got offered my Equity card by joining the original cast of *We Will Rock You* in Las Vegas. After nine incredible months with the show, I returned home to New York City and was once again back in the studio training. While studying at Broadway Dance Center, I was introduced to a teacher named Andy Blankenbuehler. The energy in his class was electric, and his style and choreography felt like they were made for me. At the time he was performing in *Man of La Mancha* on Broadway but had begun transitioning from performer to teacher and choreographer. As I took more and more of his classes, we built a relationship where he supported and challenged me not just as a dancer, but as an artist. He quickly became more than just my teacher, he was my mentor.

Andy invited me to audition for *Waiting for the Moon*, an original Frank Wildhorn musical that he was choreographing at the Lenape Regional Performing Arts Center in New Jersey. After a successful audition, I booked the show that would grant me the first opportunity to work alongside Andy as a professional. Andy's vision demanded some of the most intricate and athletic choreography I had ever performed on stage. It shifted between high-energy theatrical jazz, complicated tap routines, traditional waltzes, and the explosive joy of the Charleston. It required me to use all the skills and technique I had learned through my years of training. Getting to work alongside Andy in a professional capacity helped develop our relationship even further and would later prove to be extremely valuable.

With another credit under my belt, I returned to New York City and was once again in the grind when I auditioned for the original Broadway production of *Mary Poppins*. The process not only went on for weeks but was also one of the most demanding I had ever experienced, with endless rounds of ballet, jazz, and tap, and of course, the stressful acting and singing calls. I continued to make it through multiple callbacks, bringing my dream of performing on Broadway closer to becoming a reality. The final callback was like a scene lifted directly from *A Chorus Line*. We auditionees were all on stage dancing for our lives while the creative team was seated in the darkness of the theatre speaking to us over the "god mic." I poured everything I had into this final moment hoping this would be the show that gave me my Broadway debut. Once the final callback was over, the all too familiar "waiting game" began again.

A couple of weeks later the crushing blow arrived when I received the dreaded phone call: I had not been cast. With this being the closest I had ever been to booking a Broadway show, the rejection hit me harder than I had ever experienced before.

The ups and downs of auditioning was taking its toll on me, and my personal experience with *Mary Poppins* took quite some time to shake off. During this period, I started thinking about exploring other creative opportunities. I thought back to the times I had been in the room helping people create as well as my own experiences directing and choreographing shows at Interlochen. I realized it was during these creative processes that I felt most fulfilled and decided that this is what I should explore further.

I reached out to Andy Blankenbuehler for advice hoping to get his insights into transitioning from performer to creative. To this day, I will never forget what he told me: to be taken seriously as a creative, I needed to be 100 percent committed. He cautioned me against dipping my toes in the creative waters and then retreating to perform, warning that such inconsistency would render me forgettable, especially with me being so young. After doing some serious soul searching, my answer became clear: I was ready! I met with Andy again and explained my readiness and offered my assistance if he ever needed it. He told me he was seeking an assistant for the musical adaptation of the film *It's A Wonderful Life*, titled *A Wonderful Life*, directed by James Brennan, set to premiere at Paper Mill Playhouse in New Jersey and asked if I would be interested. I immediately jumped at the opportunity and said "YES"! That affirmative "yes" was the beginning of the new chapter that I was seeking . . . a career in theatre as a creative.

As you can see, my journey has been marked by both highs and lows. While many people speak about how rewarding and inspiring the 'ups' can be, few prepare you for the reality of the 'downs.' We are often taught that success will follow if we take the right steps, yet no one truly shows you how to face the inevitable 'no'—how to process it, learn from it, and, most importantly, move forward without taking it personally. My early years were filled with rejection and profoundly challenging moments—experiences that forced me to question everything I was doing. Yet through it all, my passion for theatre never wavered. Each 'no,' though painful, ultimately guided me forward, fueling a determination that pushed me to work harder and want it even more.

I hope that understanding my journey will provide insight for what's to come. Off we go!

What Is the Difference Between an "Assistant" and an "Associate"?

The distinction between an "assistant" and an "associate" is frequently a source of confusion, largely because these roles lack official, universally accepted definitions. Instead, their scope is defined by the unique demands of the director or choreographer and project at hand.

An **assistant**, typically brought into a production during its initial creative period, serves as a crucial yet often subtle presence hired directly by the director or choreographer. Although constantly present in the room, observing, absorbing, and offering support, the assistant is characteristically less vocal than the lead creative team and is there to facilitate when told how. They will help document what is being done during the early pre-production process and will occasionally serve in an administrative-like capacity. Once in rehearsals, their engagement tends to be less hands-on with the performers themselves, and their responsibilities usually come to an end once the production has officially opened.

An **associate**, by contrast, operates with a broader, deeper sense of authority. Working intimately alongside the director or choreographer, they assist in developing not just concepts, aesthetics, and direction and choreography, but also often delve into crucial production logistics. Far more present in the rehearsal room, they frequently take on significant responsibility running rehearsals, stepping in seamlessly when the director or choreographer's attention is required elsewhere. Crucially, their commitment extends well beyond opening night; associates typically remain vital to the show's day-to-day maintenance, playing a pivotal role in re-casting, upholding the show's integrity, and ensuring the successful roll out of the production moving forward, should that happen. They are the comprehensive right-hand from inception through its ongoing life.

Ultimately, although these distinctions provide a general framework, the precise duty of each role remains fluid, always adjusting to the specific needs of the director or choreographer you are working for. Whether in an assistant or associate position, good communication is crucial. It builds trust, fosters understanding, and enables collaboration by clearly sharing information and feelings, reducing conflict, improving problem solving, and strengthening relationships. It's the foundation for connecting with others, achieving goals, and ensuring everyone feels heard and aligned.

Richard J. Hinds rehearsing the national tour of *Elf*.
Credit: Katie Mollison

It is important to note that starting off as an assistant is a likely step on the way to transitioning to an associate. Although it is certainly possible to move directly into an associate position, the skills cultivated as an assistant significantly enhance your preparedness and success in the more advanced role. Therefore, although not always a mandatory prerequisite, this initial phase is undeniably a beneficial one.

Whether serving as an assistant or an associate, you must remember you are first and foremost, an extension of the director or choreographer. Your work and presence are a direct reflection of their vision, their aesthetic, and their leadership. This demands a profound level of selflessness; you are not there to seek the main credit, but rather to meticulously support, uphold, and actualize another artist's creative vision. Every instruction given, every nuance observed, and every challenge solved must be approached through the lens of the primary director or choreographer's intent. Embracing this mindset is paramount to becoming an invaluable collaborator.

I have asked several other associates *"What do you consider to be the definition of an Associate Director and/or Associate Choreographer"?*

- ***Lou Castro – Associate Choreographer – DEATH BECOMES HER: Broadway***
  "The skill set required for this position include helping create, innovate, organize, execute, address issues, and navigate roadblocks that may come up during the creative process. This position also requires patience, understanding, compassion, and empathy for everyone on the creative team, stage crew, and cast. It's both an honor and responsibility to be in this very important position. Associates often take over driving our department when our superiors are not in the room. We are in essence the department secretary, point person, and sometimes the collaborative driver. Since performance art inhales and exhales on a daily basis, you also have to make sure the material that was originally created doesn't stray too far away from its original intent and artistic integrity."
- ***Sarah Parker – Associate Choreographer – CAMELOT: Lincoln Center***
  "To me, the job of an Associate Director and/or Associate Choreographer is to help bring the lead director and/or choreographer's vision to life. That looks different for every person and every project. Some directors/choreographers might need you to take a lot of notes, maintain a thorough book of blocking and formation charts, help them remember changes that were made, and be in charge of all logistical details needed to communicate with other design departments. Other directors/choreographers might want more of a creative collaborator and will want their associate up on their feet beside them, contributing to the creative ideas, offering suggestions, developing movement, and actively helping them problem solve. As the associate, it is your responsibility to evaluate what kind of assistance your leader is looking for in the moment and deliver that in a way that allows them to solely focus on connecting with their actors and creating their best product."
- ***Rickey Tripp – Associate Choreographer – HELL'S KITCHEN: Broadway and First National Tour***
  "As an Associate Choreographer of fifteen years, I fully understood that my role was to be an extension of the choreographer in helping them be their best version of themselves in every aspect of their creative process, by upholding and protecting the integrity of their choreographic voice and vision, while trying to be two-steps ahead of them. And to fully support and even challenge the choreographer in their choreographic endeavors. And as an associate, you serve as a liaison between the choreographer and all other departments but mainly and for certain with the director and cast. It's vital to build healthy and respectful relationships for all to co-exist and reach their goals."
- ***Travis Waldschmidt – Associate Choreographer – CHESS: Broadway***
  "As an Associate Choreographer, you support the lead choreographer in crafting, teaching, refining, and maintaining the movement vocabulary and storytelling of the production. It all

comes down to the details and preserving the choreographer's artistic identity and style. Associates also run understudy rehearsals where you teach all the covers, including swings, for their new roles in case of vacation or illness. The longer a show runs, people will eventually get ill, hurt, and need time off, so it's very important for the associates to make sure the covers are well prepared. Speaking of longer runs, another job of an Associate Choreographer is to clean, maintain, and even adjust choreography as needed. Whether that's helping create split tracks, which means building a show where there's not enough coverage to have a full ensemble, or running brush-up rehearsals, your role is there to maintain the integrity of the show. All in all, the Associate Choreographer helps the choreographer build production numbers/transitions and then becomes its caretaker. Ensuring clarity, cohesion, and excellence throughout the life of the show."

- ***Voltaire Wade-Green – Associate Choreographer – RAGTIME – Lincoln Center***
  "To me, an Associate Choreographer is the bridge that supports both the cast and the creative team. I focus on offering help where it's most useful and stepping back when it keeps the choreographer's perspective clear. Every choreographer works differently, so the support changes from show to show."
- ***Lizz Picini – Associate Choreographer – The Muny***
  "I firmly believe that the responsibility of an Associate Choreographer, and/or Associate Director is to 'fill the gap.' An associate must remain flexible, willing, attentive, open-minded, committed, present, and engaged, in order to fully provide support at any given moment in any realm. Whether the associate is center stage, fully leading the room, or quietly, subtly taking notes, ego is left at the door in order to better/strengthen the production and process as a whole"!

"creative collaborator"
"be an extension"
"fill the gap"
"maintain the integrity"
"problem solver"

If a definitive definition were to be made, it would likely be composed of these common phrases. An associate must first and foremost be a "creative collaborator," functioning as a trusted sounding board for the creative they are working alongside, of knowing when to listen and when to bring ideas to the table. Their essential responsibility is to "be an extension" of that creative and represent them with the utmost respect, making sure every decision they make is with their creative leader's best interest in mind. They must be malleable to "fill the gap" at any given moment when needed from quickly writing down blocking in real-time to stepping up and running the room in the absence of their lead creative. Once the show is up and running, their role transitions to a management position making sure to "maintain the integrity" of the original vision and ensure it is never compromised. An associate must be capable of being a "problem solver," possessing the balance of artistic sensitivity and practical discipline to navigate challenges that arise. These phrases capture some key attributes needed to be an associate.

PART ONE
PREPARING FOR THE JOB

Do Your Research

As a child, whether seeing a Broadway show, the Macy's Thanksgiving Day Parade, or the Tony Awards, I was always eager to stay up to date with all that was happening on Broadway. This "detective work" was done by studying my Playbills or navigating the internet to learn the names of the directors, choreographers, composers, and designers involved. I used the internet to watch countless performance clips, making sure I was educating myself on the history of theatre, while also staying informed with what was currently happening. I had more theatre books than one can imagine and read every single one of them in detail from front to back. I became a theatre encyclopedia; I always knew what shows were playing on Broadway, who the teams involved were, what theatre each show was playing in, and who was in the cast. Had a Broadway quiz show been on television when I was a kid, I have no doubt I would have been a contestant and most likely would have won.

When you begin the journey into becoming an associate, I highly recommend you start by seeking out directors, choreographers, and projects that genuinely inspire you. If you are going to put yourself forward to join someone's team, it must be someone you hope to grow and learn from. This requires you to do your research and study any director or choreographer's body of work you would like to work alongside. Understanding their artistic voice allows you to recognize how your skills and perspective can serve as a valuable and complementary tool within their existing creative framework. Even if a specific project is the primary interest, delving into the backgrounds of the creative team attached is equally vital. This diligent research ensures that when you reach out to express your interest in being involved, you do so with an informed understanding, demonstrating not only your passion for the project but also your respect for the visionaries shaping it.

In today's digital world, the wealth of access one has to any director or choreographer's complete portfolio, including interviews, videos, and photos, allows for any aspiring associate to truly understand who they would like to work alongside. The New York Public Library for the Performing Arts' "Theatre on Film and Tape Archive" (TOFT), serves as an invaluable tool, one I have used often, actively preserving live theatrical productions through recordings of Broadway, Off-Broadway, and regional shows. You can fill out a form online, make an appointment, and then go to the library where you will be sat at a computer and given headphones. Another wonderful tool is the Stage Directors and Choreographers Society (SDC). It provides essential research opportunities and occasionally hosts Q&As with industry leaders.

Although admiring the brilliance of a show's creative team is part of it, you must also educate yourself about the inner workings of our industry. Who are the leading producers actively greenlighting projects and hiring talent on Broadway right now? Which general managers are attached with which productions? Which regional theatres across the country are presenting pre-Broadway try-outs? To truly stand out in any interview or meeting, one must be educated and understand precisely who is doing what, where, and why.

How does one gather and organize all this information without feeling completely overwhelmed? There are so many incredible resources out there and you must take advantage of them all. I frequently begin my day by scanning Playbill.com, not just for main headlines, but also utilizing its "JOBS" tab to see what creative opportunities are available. I check my inbox daily for my "Broadway Briefing" email, which is chock-full of news regarding castings, readings, reviews, and information on what's happening on Broadway, Off-Broadway, regionally, and internationally. I also pop onto my Instagram to see the headlines on publications such as *BroadwayWorld* and *WhatsOnStage*. While these are specifically the things that make up my daily routine, there are many other options out there as well to help make sure you are tapped in and have your finger on the pulse.

If you are preparing for an interview, this mandatory research must be viewed similarly to studying before a test—it is non-negotiable homework. The goal is to walk into any room completely saturated with knowledge. For example, before meeting a general manager, preparation requires knowing their current shows and identifying any creatives you might have in common. This knowledge provides instant talking points, allowing you to settle into the room with confidence and demonstrate professional preparedness. The benefit of this research is long-term: whether you secure that particular job or not, that information is now absorbed into your brain, equipping you for the next time one of those names or productions pops up.

Creating Content and Building a Reel

The initial journey into the associate world often presents young emerging artists with a critical dilemma: the lack of content needed to showcase their unique artistic identity. This reality hit me hard when industry contacts began requesting a reel, only for me to realize I had little to offer. This led me to submit to every choreographer's showcase imaginable, desperate to gather as much content as possible while also benefiting from getting to create different pieces of work. As I started putting together my submissions, my instinct, influenced by years in the competitive dance world, was to fill the studio with the most technically proficient dancers I knew, crafting pieces that showcased pristine execution, tricks, and clean lines. Yet, the consistent feedback from these submissions was all the same: *"The dancing is phenomenal, but where is YOUR voice"?* The critical question *"How do YOU tell stories through dance"?* After having been rejected from several of these showcases, I returned to the studio with a new perspective, letting the narrative lead the way, choosing storytelling over steps.

This new approach offered immediate results, culminating in the opportunity to present at *DanceBreak* founded by Melinda Atwood, a prestigious choreographer's showcase renowned for launching the careers of industry leaders such as Casey Nicholaw, Joshua Bergasse, Kelly Devine, and Lorin Latarro.

The brief was to conceptualize and choreograph two contrasting pieces: a musical theatre number, for which I chose "No Bad News" from *The Wiz*, and a second piece in any style you wanted, to which I chose to do a comedic theatre piece set to Richard Cheese's jazzy covers of "Baby Got Back" and "Welcome to the Jungle." Drawing on what I had learned, and with guidance from *DanceBreak* mentor Josh Prince, I made storytelling the top priority in both works. Knowing the caliber of industry leaders attending *DanceBreak*, I felt a strong responsibility to get it right.

Before I came up with a single step, I created a detailed storyboard, articulating a clear beginning, middle, and end for the narrative I intended to tell. With a strict four-minute time limit, every second mattered, and I wanted to make sure I was creating a story that would not be too complicated to deliver in the time allotted. This process was followed by a character breakdown, mapping out the individual arcs that would drive the piece. Once the story and its characters were completely fleshed out, the focus shifted to the movement. I studied the music, charting every eight-count and identifying specific musical gestures—crescendos, sudden stops, or key changes—that would serve as anchors for plot points in the story. This ensured that every action was enhanced by the music, allowing the story and music to work in total tandem. I then specifically focused on the movement, breaking it down section by section. I made sure nothing was arbitrary and that every step was deliberately chosen. It was this detailed approach that gave me the confidence that what I was presenting on stage was truly a story-driven experience.

Once *DanceBreak* concluded, each participating choreographer received a full set of high-resolution photos and videos capturing their work. Securing that first professional footage proved to be a genuine career catalyst. With this prestigious credit to my name, I began submitting these materials to directors, choreographers, and agents, and quickly noticed a shift in how my work was being perceived. It became clear that in this industry, technical skill alone is not enough; what truly resonates is the ability to craft a narrative, establish a distinct voice, and communicate a complete story arc. Encouraged by this response, I continued to create and refine story-driven choreography, making it my foremost priority.

Matthew Steffens, Ryan Steele, Kristina Fernandez, Al Blackstone, Evan Kasprzak, and Mindy Wallace in Richard J. Hinds *DanceBreak* piece.

Credit: Steven Rosen

So how do *you* go about gathering content for yourself? I suggest actively seeking out showcases and development opportunities wherever you are. These platforms will not just offer you a performance opportunity to show off your work, but more than that, they will allow you to flex your artistic muscles, get feedback, refine your work, and acquire the necessary content to elevate a professional portfolio. You also never know who will be sitting in that audience.

While presenting your work in these platforms will grant you high professional-quality footage, you must relieve yourself of the stress associated with feeling your materials must be "movielike quality." The impressive production value is not the most critical factor; the material itself is. Try filming your own choreography in a variety of settings . . . *be creative*! You can shoot in a bare studio or utilize the streets of New York City as a backdrop. You can alternate between dancers in simple black attire and those in full costume. Take the pressure off yourself and save your money. A video filmed on your iPhone can make just as strong an impression as something filmed by a professional videographer.

Make sure you are showing yourself off in as many ways as possible. You want a portfolio that is diverse, demonstrating versatility, which ultimately will make you infinitely more desirable to any creative. Don't get stuck doing the same thing.

The journey from accumulating material to crafting an effective reel is an artistic feat, often raising a list of questions: what is the ideal duration, what content should be prioritized, how many clips are truly necessary, and what music best underscores the compilation? Although these questions spark many opinions, I will offer my own perspective. First and foremost, I strongly suggest filming and editing everything in landscape orientation. This horizontal format (where the width is greater than the height) will most likely be how your content will be viewed. If something is filmed in portrait, the result will likely mean there will be thick black borders on either side, which is not ideal for the viewing experience. Whether the reel is viewed embedded on a website, hosted on YouTube, or presented within the confines of Instagram's video features, the standardized landscape approach will universally fit the viewer's screen best. Keep this in mind as you start generating material for your reel.

Musical Theatre Choreography Reel

When building a musical theatre choreography reel, the focus should be on showcasing your unique artistic voice and demonstrating the many ways you communicate a story through dance. To achieve this, resist transitioning too rapidly between clips. If the clips are excessively short, it can be challenging for the viewer to truly grasp your distinct language of storytelling, as the work never truly settles. If you want to feature several clips from a specific show, I find keeping those clips grouped together allows the viewer to have a clearer sense of your work related to that specific show. In my experience, a concise two to three minute reel is plenty, providing all the essential information needed without demanding too much time.

It is okay if the footage you are assembling varies in production value. Anyone viewing an aspiring associate's body of work understands that you might not have had the experience to work on highly commercial productions yet. We are not looking for flawless, high-budget production; we are looking for a compelling story. It is also worth remembering that not every show has an ensemble that will be doing a triple pirouette. Don't be afraid to showcase slightly more "basic" technical choreographic steps that still successfully highlight a story-driven narrative. Some shows require highly technical dancing, as seen in *MJ: The Musical*, while other shows are rooted more deeply in character-driven movement such as *Ragtime*.

Full recordings of your work should be available if a choreographer requests a deeper look into your body of work. If someone asks to see a fully realized number and you lack footage from a full show to pull from, I recommend choreographing to a widely recognized musical theatre song that you can put your own stamp on. Utilizing a song that offers immediate familiarity provides the viewer with crucial contextual shorthand.

Commercial Choreography Reel

For choreographers aiming to break into the world of commercial entertainment—think cruise ships, theme parks, and large-scale corporate productions—your reel needs a distinctly different strategic focus than one targeting traditional theatre. Your reel should prominently feature your innovative use of formations, showcasing your ability to create visually impactful patterns, seamless transitions, and the ability to adapt to stages of all sizes. Perhaps most important is a clear exhibition of stylistic versatility. Beyond a singular genre, a choreographer capable of delivering a wide array of styles, jazz, ballet, hip-hop, tap, contemporary, and commercial, will be incredibly valuable to any company. If this is in your comfort zone, I would highly suggest demonstrating a knowledge of partnering, encompassing everything from adagio and lifts to various ballroom and social dance techniques. Knowledge in partnering has often proven to give someone an advantage when being considered. A commercial reel needs to show you off as a dynamic choreographer with as much versatility as possible.

Similar to a musical theatre choreography reel, aim to keep this between two to three minutes, guaranteeing you are not overstaying your welcome and keeping the viewer's attention.

Director's Reel

The director's reel seems to get the best response when it features a tightly edited montage of four to five, contrasting clips, with a total runtime between two to three minutes. Similar to the reels I previously mentioned, versatility is the key selling point, requiring selections that showcase a broad spectrum of directorial command: scenes must highlight significant emotional range, demonstrating ability across various character types (from realistic drama to broad comedy, or contemporary works to classics). Crucially, the reel must lead with a strong opening clip, or brief montage, that immediately grabs attention and establishes the director's signature style. If you don't have access to clips from fully realized performances, you can again get a group of artists together and film something yourself.

Conclusion

Given the sheer volume of reels circulating online, taking the time to research and observe is invaluable. Pay attention to which reels genuinely resonate with you—what captures your interest, the kind of music that draws you in, and what holds your attention. Ultimately, a reel comes down to personal taste and how effectively it expresses your unique artistic vision. I've seen particularly compelling reels built around a strong, singular stylistic choice—such as a committed black-and-white aesthetic that heightens mood—while others achieve impact through precision and musicality, pairing sharply accented music with choreography that lands on every beat and nuance with intention.

Creating compelling content and meticulously building a professional reel is imperative to self-marketing for any creative individual. It's often the first introduction any director, choreographer, or industry creative will have to your talent. Your reel isn't just a collection of clips; it represents your artistry, skill set, and voice. It is crucial that it showcases you in your absolute best light. Never publish anything you wouldn't want permanently associated with your professional image. Be sure to regularly update your reel with fresh, current content, ensuring it remains an accurate display of your ongoing professional work. You should post your reel on every platform you have (Instagram, YouTube, website) so it is easy for any creative to find and becomes part of your digital footprint. It will also make it easier to send to a creative if requested based on the platform they inquire from. Some want quick and easy viewing on Instagram and others prefer a link they can catalog into their "potential associates" folder.

Building content for a reel is collaborative endeavor and will utilize the talents and time of many artists. As they too are always looking for ways to generate new content to promote themselves, I always allow artists to post anything we create on their personal reels and across their social media platforms, making sure that appropriate tagging and credit is provided. This allows both parties to get something out of this. By them posting your material on their website and social media platforms, there is a potential to reach an even larger audience.

Creating an Online Presence

The heavy lifting of generating content and building a reel is only the first half of the equation; the next phase is establishing a strategic and functional online presence. Directors and choreographers routinely conduct internet searches to quickly gather who an artist is and what they have to offer beyond a submitted resume. Your digital footprint, including a website and social media platforms, will ultimately dictate initial first impressions. Many artists find value in separating their personal and professional lives online to retain privacy. Remember that anything posted publicly is visible, permanent, and holds the potential to persuade (or dissuade) a creative's judgment about your character or professionalism. By actively using your website, Instagram, TikTok, and other platforms such as X, to your advantage, you ensure that when industry eyes begin their search, they immediately encounter a polished, accessible, and carefully crafted depiction of you and your talent.

Instagram

This platform is arguably the most useful when looking to see an array of somebody's work and to get to know a bit about them and what personal connections you might have in common. For me, through my account (@richardjhinds), I display my body of work by featuring videos from class, rehearsals, and performances as well as photos and announcements for upcoming classes and auditions. This immediate catalog of content allows followers and potential creatives to look at my body of work in a quick and efficient way, and can allow them to make informed decisions without extensive research. Although I still use it to promote myself today, I find it equally useful for evaluating future creatives I might consider working with myself. To grab viewers' attention, features like "pinning" your reel or other videos that show you off best ensure that the highest-caliber work is immediately visible at the top of the profile, saving viewers from having to take a deep dive.

Make sure to carefully think about how you want to use your Instagram account. The first step is to decide whether to merge your personal and professional lives or maintain separate accounts. If unrestricted self-expression is important to you, consider a private personal account, which offers you complete freedom to post with no judgment. Having a combined personal and professional presence means that every post, from casual snapshots to show reels, contributes to how you are being perceived by potential creatives. Although a completely private online presence might seem safe, it can also make you appear inaccessible in an industry that thrives on connection.

I find it helpful to have your contact information and agent representation listed in your profile. This is also a great place to highlight what specific project you might be working on at the moment and allows you to tag that particular show or theatre. Linking your website and email to your Instagram page is another way that makes it easy to reach you. Be sure to check your messages often, both in the "primary" folder as well as the "requests," so you can respond in a timely manner and to make sure nothing gets lost.

Although Instagram is a great tool for creatives to look into your body of work, it is also a great way for you to look into theirs. Following them, tagging them if you attend one of their shows, reaching out and introducing yourself; these are all viable ways to use this platform to connect with creatives who you would like to potentially work with. Social media platforms are specifically there to interact with others and create online communities, so don't be afraid to use them. Instagram is possibly the most valuable tool out there to connect with people in the industry.

TikTok

Although structurally not dissimilar to Instagram, this tends to feature shorter videos and thrives on trends and speed, making the ability to gather a substantial following considerably easier here. For artists, this tool can be quite successful; singers, dancers, composers, and writers can showcase their specialized skills, gain traction, and build an audience at a rapid pace. This platform is without a doubt a popular one, as it has made absolute stars out of people. For creatives, I find this platform doesn't showcase directors or choreographers in theatre as clearly. It simply does not lend itself to a detailed insight about an artist's larger body of work, making it not as widely recognized when seeking to learn about a potential creative's portfolio.

YouTube

For creatives looking to host content with a longer duration, this platform is incredibly useful. Although I acknowledge that YouTube channels may not generate the immediate, high-volume "foot traffic" like Instagram or TikTok, its strength lies in its format and the ability to post videos with no time constraints. For a director or choreographer, this means having the ability to accumulate a wide spectrum of work, from quick reels to fully realized performances, all contained in one place. One easy link directs viewers to a single hub where they can access your complete body of work, allowing them to easily jump between videos. If posting longer videos that you don't necessarily want to be available to the public, consider using other sharing platforms such as Vimeo, which will require viewers to enter a password.

Website

For any creative professional seeking to market themselves effectively, the single most valuable tool is a dedicated personal website containing all your materials in a cohesive, organized portfolio, making it incredibly easy for anyone to navigate and access. A website provides you with total control over how your brand is presented, ensuring your artistic voice and professionalism are articulated exactly as you intend. As someone who is constantly on the lookout for promising associates, I find this incredibly helpful; once I've been sent to someone's website, I can quickly and comprehensively grasp their experience, understand their creative voice, and assess their overall skill set. There are many ways to create one's site whether you choose a do-it-yourself builder or opt to invest in hiring a design company. Regardless which you use, ensure your site is accurate, polished, and always up to date.

Here are some things I believe to be vital to a successful website.

- **About Me:** A page that serves as an opportunity to let the viewer know about you on a more personal level through your own voice, often accompanied by pictures. You can talk a bit about your history and career in a very conversational way that gives the viewer a real flavor of who you are.
- **Resume**: An industry standard document that lists all your credits, venues, and creative collaborators. If marketing yourself as a performer and a creative, best to separate these two resumes. It makes it clearer for the viewer to know exactly what capacity you worked on a show.

Richard J. Hinds' website (www.richardjhinds.com).

Credit: Stage Door Designs www.stagedoordesigns.com

- **Reel:** A short video compilation showcasing your work and creative vision. This should either be embedded directly onto your site or be linked through easy navigation.
- **Multimedia:** A section that allows you to present photos and videos exactly as you wish them to be viewed, giving proper credit where needed. This is a great way to show your work on specific shows in a more fleshed out way than a reel. It helps give the viewer better insight of how you approach a specific show in its entirety.
- **Reviews:** Though not needed, this can be a great way to show how your work has been received and can be organized chronologically by show or scattered throughout the site. Positive reviews from major publications can carry significant weight and help offer you some credibility.
- **Contact:** A page that clearly supplies agent information or personal details if you are self-represented. This can also be a great place to have links directing traffic to all other social media platforms.

I suggest keeping your site streamlined to avoid overwhelming visitors and to ensure a focused and impactful presentation of your work. A cluttered or overly complex design can make it difficult for viewers to find the information they need, ultimately putting them off. An easy to navigate site allows your work to shine and will keep the viewer engaged.

Appropriate Credit

No matter what platform you are posting content on, make sure everything is credited appropriately. When posting content from class, you should credit the song, the studio, and videographer. If posting content from a performance, clearly label the production, your role, the venue where the work was staged, and the videographer. Appropriate credit is even more important when you are posting content that you were an assistant or associate on. You must obtain permission from the creative you worked with to post the video, and they should be clearly credited acknowledging their ownership. Beyond demonstrating strong ethical principles, this attention to detail when labelling allows the viewer to instantly understand the scope of your work. Detailed credit could offer networking potential: a viewer might have a direct affiliation with a creative or venue they see listed prompting them to reach out to gain further information regarding your work.

In today's world, the issue of intellectual property (IP) and copyright is an incredibly sensitive topic, I know first-hand having had to deal with my IP being stolen in Spain, Mexico, and a prominent musical theatre university in America. The rule remains clear: under no circumstances should you post or feature content for which you do not have explicit permission. Conversely, to protect your own future work, make sure any original footage you upload is labelled clearly as *your* IP and should clearly state when it was uploaded. This measure will potentially protect you in the future should you require it.

Creating Relationships

The path to securing a role as an Associate Director or Choreographer is rarely found through a traditional audition process. Unlike performers who can showcase their talent in an audition, this journey is almost exclusively built on relationships; it's about who you know. A majority of associate positions are filled through trusted networks and personal recommendations. This then leads to the question: "*How does one build these vital connections*"? A piece of advice I received early on was the simple truth that *"everyone has had someone who has given them an opportunity so don't be afraid to reach out."* The key is navigating the fine line between making a professional inquiry and becoming an annoyance. From my own experience, both as someone who sought opportunities and now as someone who receives these submissions, I will list a few tools that I have found to be incredibly beneficial.

Emails

Reaching out directly via email serves as a great initial introduction to directors and choreographers. With most creatives maintaining strong online presences, be it personal websites or active social media, they are more accessible than ever, making a personalized email for you to introduce yourself very achievable. Avoid the common pitfall of a "cut and paste" approach, as these are incredibly impersonal and read quite flat and uninspired. Instead, articulate precisely why you are reaching out to *them* specifically, what your intentions are, and why you believe building a relationship with *this particular creative* aligns with your artistic aspirations. Remember, less is often more; busy industry professionals appreciate directness, so get straight to the point. If you share a mutual contact, lead with that mention, as it instantly establishes a personal connection and lends credibility to your introduction. Crucially, include all accessible promotional materials—your website and social media links provide a quick snapshot of your work—and always attach your resume. Don't be discouraged if your resume isn't yet filled with a large amount of credits; everyone starts somewhere, and everyone understands that. Finally, prepare yourself with patience and realistic expectations. Directors and choreographers operate on notoriously demanding schedules, so an immediate response can be rare. Allow a few weeks to pass, and if silence persists, a single, follow-up email is usually appropriate, but then it's best to leave it at that.

Here is an example of an email I received from Josh Zacher.

Hi Ricky!

Josh Zacher here—congratulations on your successful run of Elf and what appeared to be a prolific year writ large! Happy New Year!

I recently closed McCoy Rigby's production of Disney's The Little Mermaid, where I served as the Associate Choreographer, restaging director, and dance captain.

Tom McCoy mentioned that you'll be directing Come From Away this fall at LMT. If you're looking for an associate on this, or any of your upcoming projects, I would love to be considered. Collaborating with you has been a long-time goal of mine, and as I prioritize transitioning more fully behind the table in 2025, it feels like the perfect time to connect.

In March, I'll be associate directing a workshop in the city, but beyond that, my year is still taking shape. For your reference, I've attached my resumes and headshot, and you can also see what I've been up to on my website.

Regardless, I'm wishing you all the best in the year ahead and continued success with your projects!

Sincerely,
Josh

My response.

Hey Josh!

So good to hear from you and congrats on everything. I've been seeing your choreography on Instagram (and your website) and it looks fabulous. I know the transition from performer to choreographer isn't always easy but you're nailing it!

I will definitely keep you in mind for future projects as I have a very busy 2025 coming up and will need some support. I will also be doing tons of pre-pro so even if an associate position doesn't work out, I would love to be in a room with you.

I'll keep you posted! Have a GREAT 2025!

Ricky

I stayed in touch with Josh and when I was asked to choreograph *La Cage aux Folles* at The Muny, he was fresh on my mind and felt like a perfect fit. I scheduled a meeting for us to get to know each other and it was quickly clear that we would be creatively compatible. I offered him the job and he lived up to every expectation I had of him. It was that simple email that put him on my radar.

Taking Classes

Many industry professionals, myself included, utilize teaching at renowned studios such as Steps on Broadway, Broadway Dance Center, Pineapple Dance Studios, and The Manor LDN as platforms to scout potential collaborators. For a choreographer seeking an associate, observing a dancer in this live setting provides invaluable insight. The classroom allows choreographers to directly assess not just technical proficiency, but crucial elements such as movement quality and how well an individual interprets and embodies their specific choreographic style. The ability to approach a creative after class, offer an introduction, and engage in a brief conversation fosters an immediate connection that is much more personal than an email and allows them to put a face to the name. Although it's natural to feel a touch nervous in these situations, try to be as natural and relaxed as possible; this brief interaction offers choreographers a genuine glimpse into your personality. Keep it concise—think of it as a quick "hello." Most choreographers will be heading from class to their next engagement and you never want them to feel they are being held hostage.

Beyond these studios, there are multiple companies out there dedicated to offering masterclasses led by established creatives across various disciplines. These sessions come in many different formats, each designed to offer unique insights and opportunities. Here are some examples:

- A "show-specific" workshop where you learn material from that show taught by the director or choreographer firsthand or an associate.
- A masterclass where you bring in your own material and perform in front of creatives who will give you on-the-spot feedback.
- An intensive that spans over several days introducing you to multiple directors and choreographers, allowing you to train with them directly in a classroom environment.

These opportunities can be found by doing a simple online search or by browsing social media. Usually these masterclasses and workshops will be wrapped up with a Q&A offering a direct dialogue between you and the teacher. Make sure you are prepared as this is a perfect opportunity to ask questions to gain more knowledge from the specific creatives you are working with.

Whether taking a dance class or attending a workshop, a face-to-face encounter will certainly help build a relationship and allows for an immediate one-on-one connection. Once you have established this, a prompt and thoughtful follow-up email is highly recommended. Make sure to remind the creative exactly where you met to help them connect the dots. This email will allow you to open a dialogue and express your interest in the possibility of working together in the future in whatever capacity they might see fit.

Shadowing/Pre-production

The prep period offers a unique opportunity for creating creative relationships and exhibiting your skills as a collaborator. Should you learn that a creative—be it a director, choreographer, or associate—has a project on the horizon, consider reaching out to offer your services, either to *shadow* or to join their team for *pre-production*.

Shadowing involves being invited into the room as a spectator, a "fly on the wall" during the initial creative explorations. Alternatively, being a part of the pre-production team means offering yourself as a participating body in the room, offering a more hands-on experience. Either option will allow you to be directly in the room with the creative you are looking to build a relationship with. Being invited into this prep period will not only provide you with a real-time view of *how* a show is built, but it will also give the creative a glimpse into your ability to help facilitate developing direction and movement. This period is often the most direct path to a future partnership; many associates I have successfully brought onto major projects began their journey by collaborating and playing alongside me during these vital pre-production sessions.

A pre-production crew is typically used to help flesh out different moments within a show. Whether it's a specific dance sequence, a complicated scene, or even a transition, these artists provide the necessary bodies to fully realize these moments. Often, these participants are selected by the director or choreographer from their existing network. Other times, these can be the actual performers who will be participating in the show. I would say most of the time, the group assembled for pre-production is a mix of both. These artists play a crucial role in the developmental phase of any show and allow the creatives to work closely with them to build these specific moments.

I frequently use platforms such as Instagram and Facebook to post when I am looking for dancers to join me for pre-production. Although participating in this capacity rarely involves financial gain, never underestimate the sheer value of simply *being in the room*. The connection you will create with the creative you are working with during these rehearsals is invaluable. It will also provide you an opportunity to meet and connect with other artists outside your inner circle. While doing pre-production for *La Cage aux Folles* at The Muny, I invited more than twenty dancers to join me during this process, many of whom I had never worked with in this capacity before. Not only have I gone on to recommend several of these dancers for performance and creative jobs, but I have expanded my rolodex of potential associates.

No matter what steps you take to connect, it is crucial to enter these processes with realistic expectations. Most directors and choreographers already have a trusted associate, therefore, an immediate opening is unlikely. By making a positive, professional, and memorable impression in any one of these processes it allows you to position yourself at the forefront of their mind for the future. Then, should an endeavor arise and an opening finally occurs, your name is already familiar, significantly increasing your chances of a potential collaboration.

Getting the Job

Building a professional network is invaluable for creating opportunities. Success often relies on the connections you have, but also on timing—being in the right place at the right time. By sharing these specific stories of how I landed key roles that shaped my career, I will be able to explain exactly what I mean.

High School Musical (North American tour)

My first encounter with Lisa Stevens was while auditioning for the regional premiere of *High School Musical* at Atlanta Theatre of the Stars, under the direction of Jeff Calhoun who I had previously met during my time at Broadway Theatre Project. After several rounds of callbacks, I was gutted to not book the show. The Atlanta production received amazing reviews and it was announced that Disney would be producing a North American tour shortly thereafter of this specific production. In between its initial Atlanta premiere and the tour was the time I started to focus on auditioning less and more specifically on the creative side of things. I saw Lisa was having an audition for an industrial she was directing and choreographing, which included a brief rehearsal process in New York City and a quick tech and single performance out of town. I would say the whole contract was no more than two weeks. It was exactly the kind of opportunity I was seeking—short-term, flexible, and leaving me available to pursue upcoming creative prospects. What made it even more appealing was the chance to work with Lisa again, whose collaborative approach I had greatly appreciated during the *High School Musical* audition process at Atlanta Theatre of the Stars.

After booking this contract, I became quite close with one of the principal actors involved in the industrial who knew Lisa previously having worked with her on *Bombay Dreams*. I explained to him my ambition to transition towards choreography and wanting to take on more creative roles. He suggested I tell this to Lisa, who was still relatively new to the New York City theatre scene and was actively expanding her pool of associates. I took this advice and emailed Lisa expressing my interest of being an associate for any future projects she might have. She responded quite quickly and revealed she had an immediate opening: her previous *High School Musical* associate had just booked another job, leaving this position open for the North American tour. It felt like kismet and before I knew it, the contract was signed and I was officially the Associate Choreographer for the very show I had once auditioned and been cut from. It was my connection to Lisa and sending that email at just the right time that helped me secure this opportunity. Had I waited only a few days, that position would have been filled and I would have completely missed out on the job that put me on the map as an "Associate Choreographer." I would go on to serve as the associate for the UK tour, the Australian company, and a second North American tour.

Coincidentally, early in the run, one of the actors sustained an injury, requiring an immediate replacement to step in during his recovery period. The company approached me with the request, and before I knew it, I was back on stage performing and would go on to become the "vacation swing" for the show. I would join the tour for sporadic weeklong engagements throughout the run while people went on vacation but was never required to be there full time. This allowed me to itch the performance bug that hadn't completely left me yet. I truly felt like I was having my cake and eating it too: I was able to still be the associate *and* I also got the thrill of popping in and performing every now and then. Thank you, Lisa!

> **Lesson learned: Don't be afraid to reach out to people. That singular email launched my entire career as an associate. When you specifically reach out to someone you have a relationship with, your reputation and skill will precede you, making it far easier for them to consider you as a potential collaborator. Take risks. Sometimes the only thing standing between you and your next big opportunity is the courage to hit send.**

Newsies (Broadway)

My involvement with the stage production of *High School Musical* ended up being much more than just a credit on my resume, it reunited me with its director, Jeff Calhoun, who I had studied with at Broadway Theatre Project. During the Chicago opening of *High School Musical*, Jeff approached me about filling the role of Associate Director for *High School Musical: The Ice Tour.* His longtime associate, Coy Middlebrook, was moving to Los Angeles and transitioning to film and television, which made this position available.

This production would draw creatives from both the stage show and the massively successful Disney film, connecting Jeff Calhoun and his team with Kenny Ortega and his. I accepted the job and flew to Florida to launch not one, but three touring companies at the same time. Jeff and I hit it off and I had clearly proven myself, as from there, I became a permanent member of Jeff's creative team. This partnership included us working on many subsequent productions together including the national tour of Dolly Parton's *9 to 5* and Deaf West's production of *Pippin*.

Then came the opportunity that would redefine my career: *Newsies*. Disney approached Jeff to direct a stage adaptation of the beloved 1992 film at Paper Mill Playhouse, with the goal of creating a definitive version for the stage that could later be licensed for amateur productions. While Jeff came to the project with fresh eyes—having been less familiar with the original film—I had grown up with *Newsies* and knew it inside and out. This dynamic allowed us to strike a balance between reimagining the material and honoring its roots. The production at Paper Mill Playhouse proved to be a critical triumph. The energy surrounding the show was palpable, yet despite its success, its future remained uncertain.

While directing and choreographing a production of *Fame* in Macau, China, I received a call from Jeff telling me that *Newsies* was going to Broadway for a limited engagement. After five years since I had accepted my first job as an associate, I would be making my Broadway debut, not as a performer but as an Associate Director. I remember sitting in the audience on opening night. As the house lights dimmed and the overture started, I reached for my mother's hand and started crying. I couldn't have imagined a more perfect way to arrive on Broadway. This is yet another example of how my work ethic and professionalism opened the door to this opportunity with Jeff. Also, being in the right place at the right time to fill the vacant "Associate Director" position on his team offered me a multitude of opportunities.

Lesson learned: Maintain good working relationships. The secret to Jeff and I's success: I never allowed myself to take a single project for granted. Trust is not given but continuously earned. On every project I continued to prove my value, which inspired Jeff to want to continue collaborating. Our journey was not without its unavoidable ups and downs, however, one crucial element never changed: my dedication and unwavering respect for Jeff as a friend and mentor.

Steve Fickinger, Jeff Calhoun (director), and Richard J. Hinds during rehearsals for *Newsies* at Paper Mill Playhouse.

Credit: Paper Mill Playhouse

Come From Away (Broadway)

I first met Kelly Devine while working on the Off-Broadway musical *Frankenstein* starring Hunter Foster. I was serving as the Assistant Director to Bill Fennelly, and Kelly was the choreographer. The budget offered no Associate Choreographer, so when Kelly learned I had a dance background, she asked if I would assist her during some rehearsals and tech. We hit it off instantly. Although our time together was short, the show only ran for twenty-five previews and forty-five performances, we quickly created a friendship that would go on for years to come.

Shortly after, I received a last-minute call from Kelly. She was directing and choreographing *The Happy Embalmer* for the New York Musical Festival (NYMF) and had unexpectedly lost her associate needing a replacement to start—tomorrow. It was perfect timing; I was in New York City and available, and I immediately agreed. The next day, I walked into a rehearsal room filled with seasoned pros, including Tituss Burgess, Daniel Reichard, and Megan Sikora. Kelly handed me a script and score and informed me she had to leave immediately for a tech rehearsal for *Memphis* on Broadway. She asked me if I would clean the opening number and off she went. Standing there with my script, which I had never read, having never heard a note of the music, and certainly never having seen the choreography, I was now leading the company in rehearsal. Taking a deep breath, I said to myself "I got this," and off we went. I very quickly proved myself to Kelly during this project and I could tell her trust in me had grown exponentially.

Following years of collaboration on shows both successful and not, she asked me to join her team for *Come From Away* at La Jolla Playhouse. After initially reviewing the script and score, I told her *"I don't get it. Who are they talking to? How can we possibly stage this when the scenes move so fast"?* She explained the concept that director Christopher Ashley and her were planning and I was immediately hooked.

Although the show had already undergone workshops, stepping into the rehearsal room at the La Jolla Playhouse carried its own quiet pressure—I was the newcomer, trying to navigate established relationships and creative chemistry. I took time to listen, to absorb the dynamics of the team, careful to not jump in too quickly. Thankfully, I was met with openness and warmth and I quickly felt part of the team.

Early in the rehearsal process, I was aware that we were working on something incredibly special. Moving from La Jolla Playhouse to the Seattle Rep, Ford's Theatre in D.C., a concert in Gander, Newfoundland, and finally Toronto, allowed us to continuously develop and finesse the material. The official announcement that we would be transferring to Broadway happened while we were in Toronto. The extensive period of out-of-town try-outs proved invaluable, allowing us to feel confident that the version opening on Broadway was the best iteration this team could deliver. The reviews that arrived during the opening night party confirmed what we had hoped: we were a HIT. This life-changing show undeniably shaped my career.

This show required us to think outside of the box and established both Kelly and I as choreographers who could build movement specifically for actors. There were no high kicks or pirouettes. It was all story driven movement requiring every gesture to have a meaning and a purpose. It forced Kelly and I to build a new vocabulary avoiding conventional dance terminology and focusing instead on action and intention. Over nearly ten years of working on this specific iteration of *Come From Away* with some of the most brilliant actors I have ever worked with has absolutely made me a better choreographer.

Lesson learned: **Trust in yourself. That initial day at** *The Happy Embalmer* **would fundamentally pave the path forward for Kelly and I's relationship. Although the situation was slightly unnerving, I did what I had been trained to do without second-guessing myself. This taught me that my capabilities were far greater than I had imagined. My ability to show decisive leadership in a stressful environment resonated with Kelly; it not only solidified her belief in me as an associate but assured her that I was someone she could trust to handle anything, including high-stress situations.**

Richard J. Hinds outside the Gerald Schoenfeld Theatre where *Come From Away* played.

Credit: Richard J. Hinds

Company (Broadway)

While working on the West End production of *Come From Away* in London, I was able to see the critically acclaimed revival of Sondheim's *Company*, starring Patti LuPone. Upon hearing the news of the show transferring to Broadway, I immediately looked up who the choreographer was and became aware of Liam Steel. Through a network of mutual friends, I managed to secure Liam's email address and took a risk by sending him the following email:

Liam

Good afternoon. My name is Richard J. Hinds and I received your contact information from Alan Berry. I am currently the Associate Choreographer for COME FROM AWAY and recently set the show in London. I had the opportunity to see your production of COMPANY and was absolutely blown away. Congrats on the Broadway transfer. I am not sure where you are in your process, but if you are looking for a New York City associate/resident, I would love to throw my name into the mix. I am attaching my resume to this email, and you can also view more of my information on my website listed below. Thank you very much for your time, and again, congrats!

Richard
www.richardjhinds.com

Liam replied letting me know he would be in New York City for preliminary auditions and asked if we could meet for lunch. I immediately did a deep dive into his work, learning as much as I could about his style and the people we had in common. That preparation proved invaluable. What I had expected to be a brief, hour-long conversation about his needs and the show's vision turned into a several-hour discussion. Because I had taken the time to understand his work, I was able to speak with confidence and insight. We shared our histories, swapped stories about mutual collaborators, and ultimately connected over the shared physical language of *Come From Away* and *Company*—both productions that challenge actors to step outside their movement comfort zones. Within a week, that initial email paid off: Liam asked me to join him as Associate Choreographer for the Broadway production of *Company*. He later shared that the mutual collaborators he reached out to all spoke highly of me—preparation, reputation, and timing ultimately aligned to secure the job.

Lesson learned: Put yourself out there. With *High School Musical* I had a previous relationship with Lisa, but when it came to Liam, I was a complete unknown. The thought of sending that introductory email was undeniably vulnerable. *What if I'm not qualified?* The reality was, the only real harm that could come from reaching out was a bruised ego if Liam never replied. Thankfully, the outcome was the complete opposite and Liam and I quickly built a great working relationship and also became very close friends. We've gone on to collaborate on *Elf* on the West End twice, Broadway, and a North American tour—all thanks to that one vulnerable email. Sometimes the greatest opportunities and friendships begin with the simple courage to put yourself out there.

Liam Steel (choreographer), Simone Sault (UK Associate Choreographer), and Richard J. Hinds at the opening night of *Company* on Broadway.

Credit: Richard J. Hinds

The roadmap to becoming an associate is very much an individual journey. Here are some other accounts from fellow associates of how they got into the associate world and what their first job was.

- ***Danny Sharron – Associate Director – CABARET AT THE KIT KAT CLUB: Broadway***
  "I was a directing fellow at New York Theatre Workshop, and as part of that fellowship I was paired with Michael Greif as a mentor (he's had a longstanding connection with that theatre, and it's where RENT premiered before moving to Broadway). We built a relationship over the course of that year, and beyond, and when he was looking for an Associate Director for Dear Evan Hansen on Broadway, he asked if I would be interested and then connected me with the producer and general manager for a proper interview. I had done a fair amount of assistant and associate directing Off-Broadway at that point, but this was how I made the move to working on Broadway shows."
- ***Lou Castro – Associate Choreographer – DEATH BECOMES HER: Broadway***
  "During my career as a performer, I was asked by Christohper Gattelli (back then an up-and-coming director/choreographer) to dance in a few of his projects. While being in the room with him, I found it very exciting to be given the permission to have a hands-on

approach in helping create movement and shape. After a few projects, he then asked me if I would be interested in becoming part of his team as a dance supervisor for a new show called Altar Boyz*, an Off-Broadway show that played in New York City for a couple of years. He then offered me the Associate Choreographer position when the show was being mounted and produced in Seoul, South Korea. Since then, I've been one of his associates and he has given me the opportunity to work on very interesting and exciting projects. Truly, it's been an honor to be trusted in the room by him."*

- ***Travis Waldschmidt – Associate Choreographer – CHESS: Broadway***
  "My transition from performer to associate felt natural because I'd always known I wanted to be a choreographer. I had fully scratched my "performer itch," so stepping into my next chapter felt more like an evolution than a departure. Knowing that my time as a performer was coming to an end, I started to swing and dance captain with choreographers I deeply admired. This allowed me to be a part of their choreographic process and have a front-row seat into what being an associate might entail. From there, I reached out to the choreographers I'd previously worked with and shared my interest in stepping into associate roles if they ever needed additional help. I have been incredibly fortunate to work with incredible collaborators/artists and even luckier that they've trusted me to be by their side."
- ***Ashley Rodbro – Associate Director – MOULIN ROUGE!: Broadway***
  "I started as stage manager when I first moved to New York. It was a great way to have a seat at the table in the rehearsal and tech process, especially during the development of new work on bigger projects than I was directing at the time. I was always working on my own directing projects in between stage management gigs, but when I started working on Oh, Hello on Broadway *with Nick Kroll and John Mulaney (directed by Alex Timbers) as a stage manager off-Broadway, that show and that job became bigger and bigger. When the show went on to do a national tour, I became the production supervisor, and when the show was eventually going to Broadway, Alex Timbers asked me if I would join the directing team as an Associate Director and script supervisor, which was my first associate job and my Broadway debut."*

PART TWO
ON THE JOB (MUSICALS)

Preparation

The role of an Associate Director or Choreographer comes with no one definition but is rather sculpted entirely by the needs and expectations of the creative you are supporting. You will quickly learn that there is no one way to do anything and your success is measured by how effectively you work alongside your director or choreographer. Although the contract will list specific dates including auditions, pre-production, rehearsal, tech, and opening night—these dates represent only a portion of the workload. An associate will dedicate hours, weeks, or even months to an intensive prep phase working closely alongside the creative team. Some of the initial work could include detailed research and organizing this material, tracking the characters in the show scene by scene and song by song, charting formations and blocking, taking extensive creative notes: all things that will allow the entire creative team to enter the rehearsal room prepared and ready to go. During this crucial prep period is where a show's vision truly begins to materialize, offering the associate a real opportunity to contribute ideas and suggestions and help flesh out new concepts being brought to the table. Many times throughout this period the designers will join as well and start integrating their ideas and designs into the fold bringing the whole show to life. These early collaborations are crucial not just for shaping the production but also for solidifying the relationships between the entire creative team. Although these periods involve everyone collaborating and having a voice in the room, it is important to remember that between the creative you are working with and yourself, it is they who always retain the final artistic decision in your partnership.

An associate must master the art of knowing precisely when to contribute and when to listen. This isn't a skill found in any rulebook, but rather an intuitive understanding created by "reading the room" and making smart, educated choices. Tensions frequently run high during the creative process. Should a situation make you feel offended or hurt, I recommend finding a suitable, well-timed moment to articulate your feelings. The exchange of apologies is a common thread in this industry; I've offered them to countless creatives and received just as many in return. This cycle of intense creative pressure, tight deadlines, and the emotionally taxing nature of the work inevitably leads to frayed nerves and elevated tempers. Everyone operates within a high-stakes environment where the line between passionate debate and escalating frustration is incredibly fine, making clear communication essential for success.

Navigating the often uncompensated "prep period" demands complete transparency from the outset regarding your availability. From the moment you commit, clearly communicate your accessibility to your creative leader. This period often presents financial challenges for associates. Many secure flexible, short-term jobs such as teaching, judging dance competitions, or quick performance opportunities to bridge the income gap. If this preparatory phase begins to consume a significant portion of your time, it's advisable to discuss it with your director or choreographer and consider approaching the producers about compensation. Although a general fee often includes this preparatory work, prolonged periods can render it insufficient. There is no industry standard for what is an appropriate amount of time for prep included in your fee when signing your contract.

Things to be expected of you during this prep-period.

- **Production meetings.** Depending on your team, these can be weekly or monthly. They are frequently held via Zoom or Google Meet and are recorded for those unable to attend. It is important for an associate to be taking detailed notes during these meetings that they can look back at for reference should any questions come up.
- **Pre-production.** I would say one full week of pre-production including full days, 10:00 a.m. to 6:00 p.m., is standard before discussions of additional compensation should begin. During these sessions, an associate will be involved in contributing to facilitate the creative vision by actively helping to build and refine ideas. You'll also be tasked with taking meticulous notes, charting formations in real-time, and filming every moment for future reference. Yet, the workday doesn't end there. The evening hours are equally vital, where you'll be labeling, organizing, and cataloging all the day's captured content and notes. This detailed organization ensures that every piece of information gathered from the day remains clear, accessible, and ready to be used for future reference.

Furthermore, associates are often tasked with specific projects (charting, research, documenting, tracking) that can be completed on their own schedule, providing a bit of flexibility. The key to a successful pre-production period is open and transparent communication: establish a clear understanding of what the creative's expectations are and be equally assertive in communicating your own schedule and availability. Ultimately, knowing your worth and advocating for fair compensation and reasonable boundaries is crucial during this intensive early phase. For projects you anticipate requiring large amounts of your time during this prep period, I would suggest securing a negotiated day rate upfront to make sure you are compensated for your time.

I will use the 2022 West End production of *Elf* as an example of what was asked of me leading up to the first day of rehearsal. I received my initial offer and contract in the beginning of July 2022 and it outlined the following dates

Auditions: July 25–August 7, 2022
Rehearsals begin: Monday, October 10, 2022
Tech begins: Tuesday, November 9, 2022
First preview: Monday, November 14, 2022
Opening night: Thursday, November 24, 2022

My fee included rehearsals, tech, and previews, and there was an additional payment specifically for auditions.

As the process began, this was what our schedule looked like.

July 2022:

- Last week of July we had preliminary auditions Monday–Friday (averaging 10:00 a.m.–6:00 p.m.).

August 2022:

- First week of August we had final callbacks Monday–Friday (averaging 10:00 a.m.–6:00 p.m.).
- Preliminary design meetings averaging once a week lasting one to two hours.
- Choreographer Liam Steel and I held weekly meetings (sometimes in person and sometimes over Zoom), discussing preliminary ideas and concepts to make sure that any specific prop or costume needs were relayed to the appropriate departments. These meetings typically lasted two to three hours.

September 2022:

- Weekly check-in meetings with director Philip Wm. McKinley, Liam, and designers making sure everything is on track for the first day of rehearsal.

October 2022:

- October 1–October 9: two full days of choreography pre-production with a group of dancers as well as four other days of choreography prep with Liam and I by ourselves.
- October 10 rehearsals commenced.

Although my contract specifically stated dates for “auditions“ and the “first day of rehearsal,” a significant two-month gap existed between these two, a period where I was not being compensated, yet many pre-production and choreography meetings were happening. Having worked with Liam before, I knew he would be incredibly flexible putting the schedule together. His accommodating approach during this period allowed me to pursue other jobs including teaching dance classes and choreographing a pantomime, ensuring I could sustain myself financially during this gap all while making sure *Elf* was still a priority.

Had I been collaborating with someone less flexible—someone demanding strict adherence to their schedule—a conversation would have been necessary. Often, creatives involved in a project may not be aware of your contractual terms or fee structure, and they might not realize that you are not being compensated during this early prep period. If an excessive amount of time was being asked of me, my first step would be to transparently communicate my contractual situation, clarifying that these preliminary hours are being unpaid. If the workload begins to resemble a full-time commitment, I would advocate for a discussion with the producers to establish a retainer or some form of guaranteed compensation. This ensures fairness, protects my time and value, and maintains a respectful working relationship. Ultimately, no professional should be taken advantage of, and no one should find themselves losing money on a project simply because their time isn’t properly recognized or compensated.

Auditions

The Process

The audition process will be heavily influenced by the specific creative team in charge and the immediate needs of the production—whether seeking an original cast or a specific replacement. As an Associate Choreographer specifically, my role shifts greatly depending on the preferences of the lead choreographer.

In some instances, the choreographer will be extremely hands-on in the process; they will be in the room for the very first audition, demonstrating the combinations, making all preliminary cuts, and maintaining control over the initial casting. More commonly, however, the choreographer will be present in the room but will use the associate to teach and demonstrate the choreography, stepping forward when the candidates are performing in small groups to make cuts. Another extremely common approach involves the associate being responsible for making the preliminary cuts, narrowing down a vast pool of talent to a manageable group for callbacks, ensuring that all specific technical and aesthetic requirements are met before the choreographer's direct involvement. Ultimately, these differing approaches are completely decided by the creative leader's working style, and the job of the associate remains consistent: to expertly facilitate however the choreographer needs.

When an associate is also known within the industry as an educator and has a direct relationship with people coming into the audition room, this can require tough decisions to be made. Although wanting to provide everyone in the room with a positive learning experience, the reality is not everyone is going to be right for every show, which can sometimes cause an associate to feel torn. I believe it is easier to make those hard decisions earlier in the process than stringing someone along when you know it ultimately won't be a fit. An associate must consciously separate the roles: as an educator you nurture and inspire while as an associate you must serve the needs of the production with impartiality. Maintaining this boundary is not a betrayal of mentorship.

I remember a very specific experience I had. I auditioned for a Broadway-bound show and was kept for the entire day making it through multiple dance cuts, only to be told at the end of the day by the choreographer that I was not right for the show, but he specifically kept me because he enjoyed watching me dance. Although I understand the choreographer's decision to do this was well-intended, it was ultimately misleading, making me think I was getting closer and closer to booking the job. Holding onto this experience, I decided to be completely transparent with people auditioning for projects I work on, and although it may hurt initially, I find knowing the truth will prevent anyone from potentially getting their hopes up for a show I know is simply not a fit.

The casting process requires creating a space that is a level playing field for any performer who steps into the audition room. Although it is natural to recognize familiar faces, students, former colleagues, close friends, or past cast members, I believe it to be imperative to not show any favoritism. I make sure that every single person who walks through that door receives precisely the same amount of focus and attention. I never want someone to feel insecure because of their lack of a previous relationship. The success of any show is about finding the absolute best talent available, which is why I avoid letting my past relationship with someone sway me one way or another. I pride myself on treating everyone equally in the room. When evaluating someone who is new to me, I proactively reach out to at least two creatives listed on their resume to gain insight into their professionalism, work ethic, and character. This practice allows me to make informed decisions, offering me the knowledge that the auditionee I am considering comes with strong character references.

The energy you lead an audition room with will set the tone for the room. The auditionees are already navigating a nerve-wracking situation so it's helpful for those on the other side of the table to help alleviate that stress. Most of the people running the audition room, including associates, have at one point or another been performers, so they know firsthand the stress that comes with auditioning. I encourage you to make a conscious effort to foster an environment where each performer feels seen, heard, and supported. By creating a safe space people will more likely present the best version of themselves.

Richard J. Hinds running auditions for *La Cage aux Folles* at The Muny.
Credit: The Muny

While serving as the Associate Director for *Newsies,* I remember watching and learning from choreographer, Christopher Gattelli, during the audition process. On several occasions, after all the groups were done dancing, Chris would ask the entire group if anyone felt they hadn't danced their absolute best and wanted one more chance. As you can imagine, many people would raise their hand and step forward. Seeing them breathe a sigh of relief knowing they would get one more chance to prove themselves was heartening. That act of kindness and respect turned a high-pressure environment into a calmer and more relaxed one, allowing everyone in the room to walk away hopefully knowing they had done their absolute best. I have carried that practice with me, striving to create a room where, regardless of whether a performer is cast, they leave feeling they have been given every opportunity to succeed.

Taking Audition Notes

Each creative develops their own unique scoring and notating method for auditions, which efficiently allows them to recall countless individuals seen in a single day. My personal approach involves a "1–5" scoring system, where "1" signifies the lowest rating and "5" the highest, a wider range than a "1–3" scale, which I have also seen commonly used. My score is also accompanied by a single, identifying characteristic—a distinctive piece of clothing, a specific hairstyle, the presence of glasses, etc. This detail acts as an anchor, instantly jogging my memory when reviewing notes later.

Specifically in a dance call, an associate provides the choreographer with an extra set of eyes. Their observation ensures that every participant is being considered carefully, preventing any promising talent from accidentally slipping through the cracks. This extends beyond just the moment when auditionees are performing the combination in small groups. While the potential candidates are focused on learning and executing the steps, both the choreographer and associate are simultaneously observing the entire room, monitoring behavior, attitude, and overall energy. This is a vital part of the process, and behavioral notes often hold much weight in post-audition conversations. Although the team strives to cast the most technically proficient performers, their ultimate goal is identifying good, kind, and professional people who will contribute a positive energy to the rehearsal room.

When serving as an Associate Director in the audition room, I meticulously document performance details, paying close attention to whether an actor's interpretation aligns with the show's stylistic requirements. Even with a strong initial read, I usually offer at least one note to gauge an actor's adaptability and receptiveness to direction.

I want to empower you to not be afraid to use your voice in the audition room. It is totally acceptable to express concerns about potential candidates, especially if you have had a negative past experience. This isn't about personal vendettas; it's about protecting the show. No one wants to hire someone whose attitude could disrupt the collaborative spirit and hinder the creative process. Although I always want to give someone the benefit of the doubt, dismissing direct, firsthand experiences with someone's character or behavior is a disservice to the team. During auditions, individuals naturally present their best selves, making it challenging to gauge true character. Therefore, it is vital to trust your instincts and be transparent about actors who have previously been problematic. Your honest feedback is a valuable asset in making informed decisions that benefit the entire production. If you have reservations regarding a specific actor, I suggest voicing those concerns sooner rather than later. I promise you the creative team will be grateful for this information.

Original Casts

Building a show from the ground up presents its own set of unique circumstances. You're often not entirely sure what you're seeking, sometimes until it stands before you, prompting that undeniable "that's it!" moment. Going into the room with this uncertainty requires an even more meticulous approach to note-taking; every detail taken regarding someone's audition will be essential when sifting through later, especially since candidates aren't fitting a specific mold of a preexisting role.

Often, it's a performer's ability to understudy that keeps them in contention. A single candidate might be seen and evaluated across several days, or even weeks, making their way through several cuts, being asked to prepare different sides and musical cuts. This extended timeframe means there can be a significant lag between the initial audition and the final callback, creating a critical challenge: how does one accurately recall their specific thoughts on this person. It is this drawn-out process that reinforces the necessity of a clear, concise, and comprehensive noting system. Such a system allows you to quickly reflect on previous observations, allowing you to make informed decisions, ensuring the perfect talent is cast. Often, casting teams also film auditions, providing a valuable visual reference to review later.

For associates, the final callback can be a stressful experience. Having guided these hopefuls through multiple rounds, often spending more time with them than anyone else on the creative team, you have witnessed their growth and carry an intimate knowledge of each candidate that is beyond their mere talent. You've invested emotionally in the journey these individuals have navigated from that very first audition to this final moment. On this day, however, there will be many fresh faces on the decision-making panel, meaning all the auditionees are blank slates being judged solely on this callback. Although you still might have the opportunity to fight for someone should you feel it necessary, it can be a difficult battle to win when the rest of the panel just doesn't have that previous knowledge. One shaky audition can completely shift a person's potential chance of booking the show, causing you to feel disappointment as you have rooted for them for so long.

The final casting wrap up consistently proves to be the most fulfilling. This critical session often begins with the casting director setting a large table, carefully labelled for every principal role and ensemble track. This organization is critical, particularly for helping visualize the ensemble, where each "track" is typically defined by the specific covers that come with it, ensuring the team clearly sees how every individual piece fits into the larger puzzle. The room begins carefully reviewing each person left by this point in the casting process. The discussions, sometimes heated, begin as everyone in the room, associates included, identifies their favorite candidates for each role, sparking many different reactions to each auditionee. I have seen these deliberation periods happen quickly and other times they have taken hours. No one wants to make a rash decision, so every possible scenario is carefully discussed. That moment when everyone signs off and the cast finally reveals itself is thrilling.

After the fact, many creatives just stand and stare at the collection of headshots that now make up the company, often ending the session with a picture of those headshots to be able to reference. If a specific track has not been identified, this process could potentially start all over, however, this time in a much more condensed way as you are now looking for one specific thing.

Replacement Casts

Having worked on several long-running productions, the casting process for a replacement track is a very different process. You are looking for someone who needs to step into a pre-existing role; making the boxes that need to be checked very specific. This is where an associate truly steps into a pivotal role taking the reins, becoming the essential voice of the director or choreographer. Taking every bit of information learned during the show's original rehearsal process, the associate leads the room, working hands-on with candidates to teach choreography directly from the show or giving very specific directorial notes regarding a scene.

For a production like *Come From Away*, Associate Director Daniel Goldstein and I collaborated closely with Casting Director Rachel Hoffman at Telsey Casting. Our initial phase involved several days of in-person auditions and sifting through a significant volume of video submissions, steadily narrowing down the pool. Once we identified a select handful of potential candidates, the lead creative team would come in for final callbacks, sometimes in person and sometimes online. At this stage in the process, the creative team expects that all presented candidates have been thoroughly vetted and meet the full requirements of the show. It is important for an associate to only present people they have complete confidence can fulfill the demands of the show. Many times, this final callback is the first time the director and choreographer will see these potential candidates present material from the show. They will often lean on the associates to pass on information as to what the process has been like for these actors and who their preferred candidate would be. Casting a replacement is substantially more streamlined as the demands are much more specific, often being completed in just a couple of sessions.

Pre-production

Once the principal and ensemble cast is solidified, the creative team transitions into the essential task of creating a **scene by scene**, a document often built and managed by an associate. This involves a detailed tracking chart, which identifies every ensemble member's track and specifies their role in every scene and song throughout the entire production, creating a blueprint for the show. This becomes an incredibly useful tool to know who is available when. As stage management is often not on contract yet during this phase, associates assume crucial responsibility for maintaining this complex paperwork until the formal handover can occur, at which point stage management will work closely with the associates to make sure everything is always up to date.

Following this initial pass through of the show, the focus shifts to the "pre-production" phase with a tentative blueprint now in place to help guide the team. Although typically organizing a scene by scene comes first, it isn't necessarily always the case. Some teams prefer to start the pre-production period with a complete blank slate and let the discovery process dictate who is being used when.

The pre-production phase is a vital period in the life of any piece of theatre, serving as the creative incubator where ideas begin to take shape. During this dedicated time, the creative team comes together to collaboratively explore the artistic vision of the production. This process often involves brainstorming conceptual themes, workshopping pivotal scenic transitions, developing a unique movement vocabulary, or deeply investigating specific scenes or musical numbers. By utilizing performers as "bodies in the room," the team can begin realizing the show on its feet. Given the typically tight schedules for rehearsals, pre-production offers the invaluable luxury of time and creative freedom, allowing for risk taking, refinement, and the solidification of key elements before the full cast dives in. In essence, it is during pre-production that the foundation of the show is built.

Other things an associate might be responsible for during this period is to help create a **research folder** that will serve as an incredibly valuable tool, accumulating photos, videos, and historical articles that help visualize the world of the production. This folder helps make sure that creatives, designers, and actors all have a shared reference point, particularly essential for shows dealing with specific historical accuracy. Having had the opportunity to choreograph *La Cage aux Folles* at The Muny, this collaborative research folder was invaluable. Director Marcia Milgrom Dodge, set designer Matthew Buttrey, costume designer Bobby Pearce, and I first established an "inspirational board" using Pinterest, gathering reference images of Parisian architecture, vibrant can-can images, textures, and Art Deco motifs. This initial visual glossary sparked our creative conversations, allowing us to move toward more specific research. For my part as choreographer, I immersed myself in hours of footage of classical French can-can, studying the history and incredible intricacies of the dance form. Although the ultimate goal was to create a world unique and specific to our production, understanding and honoring the root of the dance language was incredibly important to me. When we reconvened, the team was armed with highly detailed historical and visual references that created further artistic conversations before the official design process ever began. This research folder, continuously being added to, became the indispensable root from which our show was created, serving as a brilliant educational resource that ensured the entire company understood the context that inspired our choices.

Finally, one of the biggest expectations of any associate is documenting the show through a **Blocking Bible**. This document combines the script and blocking and acts as the definitive single source for every detail of staging and choreography. Included in this document are charts that show specific formations and transitions. Most associates use **Stage Write**, an app designed for theatre to help creatives track and document all aspects of a show in a visual format. The existence of this comprehensive Blocking Bible is now considered essential for most major commercial plays and musicals, not only for maintaining artistic integrity during long runs but also for enabling seamless replication in future productions, tours, or additional companies. I will discuss these documents in much greater detail in **Documentation and the Blocking Bible**.

In Rehearsal

The rehearsal room is where months of preparation will finally pay off. As an associate, you must come into this process completely ready to go, prepared to be the first one in and the last one out, always "on" while ready to constantly support the creative you are working with throughout the day. The days are long and will be both exhausting and exhilarating. When the rehearsal day ends for the company, you will often continue into scheduling and wrap-up meetings that can sometimes extend well into the night as you continue to build and refine the show. During the rehearsal day, every director and choreographer employs their associates differently, making the ability to "read the room" the most vital skill. The associate's role is fundamentally one of support, demanding flexibility: sometimes that means standing shoulder-to-shoulder with the creative, demonstrating material directly to the cast; other times, it could mean stepping silently into the background, focusing entirely on documenting, charting, and writing down every subtle detail, always bearing in mind that the room belongs to the creative you are there to be the associate to. As the process continues, certain undertakings will fall to you. You might be asked to work privately with a cast member who is struggling picking up and needs a little extra help. Or you might be asked to lead a company rehearsal while the director or choreographer is pulled away. The associate must be ready to switch seamlessly between being there to assist or stepping into a leadership role at a moment's notice.

Richard J. Hinds rehearsing the national tour of *Jekyll & Hyde*.

Credit: Billy Bustamante

As the Associate Choreographer on *Come From Away*, my role included navigating the varying movement backgrounds and learning speeds of our cast. With Kelly Devine, the choreographer, consistently involved in the rehearsal process, I frequently stepped in to offer one-on-one time for those who needed a little extra help. My primary goal during these sessions was to create a positive, uplifting environment, ensuring that no actor felt selfconscious, frustrated, or stuck 'in their heads.' To keep things light, I found humor in the process by tapping actors on the shoulder and letting them know they were being offered a 'private lesson.' This dedicated time proved invaluable; it allowed individuals to build their confidence and refine their movement. Kelly and I had a strong working relationship, which meant that I could anticipate when and where my assistance was needed, often without discussion, and I could go into action. By staying constantly attentive to the room, I could identify moments of downtime, seamlessly pulling an actor aside for a quick session without ever disrupting the main rehearsal flow. This blend of awareness, proactivity, and always being a step ahead isn't just helpful—it's a defining characteristic that truly makes an effective associate.

Every directive, every detail of movement, and every piece of information offered by the director or choreographer should be documented in detail. These notes serve as an invaluable resource, offering a quick and reliable way to revisit specific details that may have been given hours or even days before. Comprehensive documentation acts as a crucial resource to many other departments who will lean on the associate to help provide clear and accurate information when questions arise. Your notes will also become a vital tool when training understudies, ensuring the director or choreographer's integrity remains intact. It's important to acknowledge that even with diligent notetaking, you may not always have every answer. Although this can feel vulnerable, embracing the opportunity to seek out that missing information means you will have an answer and be better equipped in the future with this knowledge.

An associate tends to become the "go-to" person, requiring you to maneuver carefully. Although this is sometimes being done simply because of efficiency—especially when a creative is busy and answers are needed swiftly—it carries the risk of making that creative feel left out. Every conversation should be relayed promptly so the creative never suspects a critical decision or discussion is happening without them. Complicating this delicate balance is the relationship with the actors, who often seek out the associate to voice concerns they are hesitant to bring directly to the creative. You receiving information before your director or choreographer can prove problematic. Some creatives are incredibly territorial about their information stream, and learning second hand that information has been shared without them can quickly become an issue. The moment sensitive or specific information is shared with you, deliver it immediately to them. This will eliminate any loose ends and ensure no one is left in the dark.

Taking and Giving Notes

Every director and choreographer will have a specific way for how they would like their **actor notes** to be taken. Whatever their preference may be, one thing remains the most important: clarity and detail. Directly asking the creative how they prefer their notes to be taken is the quickest way to ensure it is being done to their liking and avoids any discrepancies throughout the process. Although some associates find typing notes their preference, others opt for handwritten notes. I have found that most creatives I have worked with have specifically asked for their notes to be typed when running longer chunks of the show or if doing a run through. If running a short section of the show, clearly written notes usually suffice. In these instances, the team tends to go right into notes following these shorter runs, where you will pass your pad of notes directly over to the creative, making good penmanship essential. You never want your creative to be stumbling over notes that they are unable to read or understand.

As a production progresses and the cast begins to run longer sections of the show or perform full run-throughs, the importance of effective note-taking becomes even more crucial. Specificity is key when taking notes during these runs, as the gap of time between when the creative has told you the note and when they are giving it can lead to forgotten details. Your thoroughness will help

ACTOR NOTES

ACTOR	NOTE
ACT 1, SCENE 1	
GREASE	
Marjorie	Make sure when you punch your R arm down that your R shoulder is completely DS towards the audience on *"THERE AIN'T NO DANGER."* ***HIT***
Anthony	When you first enter from SL1, you are coming too far onstage. You should only go to SL6 and right now you are going to SL4.
Elyn	Is it possible for you to get to the clump a beat sooner to help with the traffic of the T-Birds running up?
Lizz	When you connect with Kenickie, take a couple more beats with him before you leave to go to the Pink Ladies. We need to see this relationship right from the beginning and it is going by a bit too fast. Find Ricky to discuss further.
ACT 1, SCENE 2	
Andrew	When you first see Miss Lynch, your entire demeanor needs to change. Throw on the charm and aim to be her star pupil.
ACT 1, SCENE 4	
SUMMER NIGHTS	
Company	When you all freeze for the first time, make sure your silhouette is a real and natural one. Some of you are too stylized and it is drawing our eye.
Matthew & Clark	When you pass the basketball back and forth, make sure it stays on the music and feels natural.
Elyn, Alec & Sam	Can you get to the table sooner? Would be great if you are sat before Danny and Sandy start singing again.
ACT 1, SCENE 5	
Rizzo, Marty, Frenchy & Jan	This scene is getting a bit too big. Anchor all these characters in a reality and be careful you don't go into "character" voices.

An example of "actor notes".

Credit: Richard J. Hinds

trigger their memory to what that moment was and will allow them to deliver that note with complete clarity.

A well-structured format is helpful to successful note-taking and should include essential details such as the actor's name or character name, the scene and song where the note applies, and a clear and concise description of what the note is. By presenting notes in this manner, the creative can easily follow along and quickly identify who the note is intended for, where in the show it takes place, and what the note is. As you become more familiar with the creative you are working with, documenting notes using their language will help in making it easier for them to decipher.

As an associate, there will be times during the rehearsal process where the director or choreographer will look to you to make sure that notes are being delivered to the actors if an official "note session" is not possible. The act of giving notes relies entirely on the relationship established between the associate and the company. Since individuals process feedback differently, it is essential to establish a clear and concise language that makes sure the note is being articulated clearly and minimizes misinterpretation. Developing this language requires an understanding of the company's dynamics and the unique needs of each actor, which will help determine the optimal moment to deliver a note. With actors juggling multiple demands during rehearsals, timing is everything and approaching them at the right moment can be the difference between a note being absorbed and acted upon, or falling on deaf ears. In the moment, associates must often make quick decisions, intuitively sensing whether a note requires immediate attention or can be given at a later time depending on the energy they are receiving from the specific actor the note is intended for.

A benefit to giving notes during the rehearsal process is that the creative team are still easily accessible. When a note is met with resistance or requires further clarification, the director or choreographer can be brought in to offer more specific guidance. As an associate, hearing the creative team elaborate on their notes will allow you to gain a deeper understanding of their intended vision. Documenting these conversations and notes can prove invaluable in the long run, as it creates a reference point that can be revisited if similar issues arise.

Once in tech and previews, actor notes are typically organized in the same fashion. However, now you'll be introducing **tech notes** and the **change log**. Tech notes is a dedicated document with notes specifically for the designers. These notes will typically be organized by department—such as set, lighting, sound, and costumes. Like actor notes, you will need to make sure you clearly label where in the show the note takes place and exactly what the note is. The change log is a document that records every creative modification made during tech and previews. With many adjustments being made as you make the transition from the rehearsal room to the stage, this document serves as a centralized reference point for actors and crew alike. For performers, who may be physically onstage and unable to jot down updates in real time, the change log becomes a vital resource that they are able to review before revisiting any moments that might have been adjusted. This document will be created daily with a clear date in the heading to help everyone keep track. I typically email this document directly to the actors myself or through stage management, and also leave a printed copy at their stations for easy access.

Whether you are taking actor notes, tech notes, or documenting the change log, it is always better to err on the side of providing too much information than too little.

During the chaotic periods of tech and previews, the creative team's attention is often pulled in many different directions, leaving them to rely heavily on their associates to deliver notes to the company in a timely and effective manner. The distribution of these notes can be done in many ways,

GREASE THE MUSICAL

TECH NOTES

LIGHTING	
SUMMER NIGHTS	Can we get more light on Danny & Sandy at the end? *"SUMMER DREAMS, RIPPED AT THE SEAMS…"*
GREASED LIGHTNING	When the dance break starts, can we get more side light on the Ensemble as they enter?
Act 1, Scene 6	When Patty enters and sits on the bleachers, she is a bit dark. Can we get more light on her?
BORN TO HAND JIVE	When the couples first start dancing, can we get more isolated pools of light around each couple? Team choreo has charts if you need to know where people are.
COSTUMES	
Frenchy	Can you shorten her Pink Lady jacket? It's a bit long.
Sandy	it?
PROPS	
SUMMER NIGHTS	Can Eugene's bookbag get more stuffing and weight put into it? It looks a little empty.
Sonny's bat	Can this look a bit more beat up? It looks too new.
SOUND	
School bell	Can this be a little louder?
Missed cue	pg. 7 **Roger:** *"Hey Kenickie."*
Missed cue	pg. 15 **Frenchie** *"Let's go Sandy."*
BEAUTY SCHOOL DROPOUT	Female ensemble vocals are too quiet. Can they be lifted?
WIGS	
Rizzo	Can you trim her bangs a little? They are getting into her eyes.
SCENIC	
Marty's house	Can we frost the window so it is not so see-through?
Gymnasium	Can there be more posters around the gym wall? Class president? Musical audition notice?

An example of "tech notes".

Credit: Richard J. Hinds

CHANGE LOG: Thursday, January 8th

SCENE/SONG	ACTOR	CHANGE
ACT 1, SCENE 1		
	Felicia	Instead of entering from SR1, you now enter from SR2 when first entering
GREASE IS THE WORD	Jessica	You will now X US of Maggie to get to the cafeteria table
GREASE IS THE WORD	Matthew	Maggie will now pass you the lunch box to take offstage with you
ACT 1, SCENE 2		
	Lori & Jill	You will now both enter at the same time as soon as Miss Lynch says *"Then move!!!!"*
ACT 1, SCENE 4		
SUMMER NIGHTS	Patrick	You are now starting the *"A-WELL-A"* choreography on the R foot
SUMMER NIGHTS	Lizz	Your new ending number is 5SL next to Rizzo
SUMMER NIGHTS	Josh & Marjorie	You are both exiting out SL2… make sure you let the lockers exit first… check in with the Dance Captain if you have any questions about this
	Matthew	Make sure you unlock the table before exiting… check in with Stage Management if you need to know where it is

An example of a "change log".

Credit: Richard J. Hinds

and the approach often depends on the specific circumstances and the individual actor's needs. When time permits, delivering notes directly to the actor in person is generally the preferred method, as it allows for a two-way conversation and immediate clarification of any questions or concerns. However, in cases where a note may require some time for reflection and digestion, sending it privately via email can be a more considerate approach, allowing the actor the opportunity to process the information without the pressure of an immediate face-to-face interaction. You can then follow-up in person the next time you are both together and open a dialogue if needed. Regardless of the method, with the creative team still actively being involved in the production, it allows an associate the option to loop them in immediately if further explanation is needed.

Once a show is open, the associate typically inherits the role of maintaining the show's artistic integrity, serving as the main voice providing notes to the cast, and no longer has the creative team there to support them. The window to distribute notes can be challenging as you are not allowed to give notes after half-hour, but that tends to be the time when most actors walk into the building. Navigating this effectively makes your relationship with the stage management team incredibly helpful, as they will become your essential pipeline for communication. When the associate cannot deliver a note personally, the stage management team steps in as the messenger, ensuring information reaches the cast. Additionally, because the stage management team watches the production every night, they too often contribute their own essential performance notes. This partnership is imperative and maintaining open communication is paramount.

Every adjustment, no matter how minor, must be shared with stage management, as even the smallest creative change can affect the way they call the show. For instance, if the stage management team is accustomed to an actor delivering a line with a certain timing and the associate asks that actor to speed it up, this seemingly small adjustment could throw off the spot where the stage manager is calling a complex scenic or lighting cue, potentially leading to a dangerous situation on stage. Therefore, the associate and stage management team are truly one cohesive unit and must always work closely together. When I am serving as an associate on a show, I always email the stage management team the notes I plan to distribute to the cast, to make sure we are constantly aligned. This allows them to be in the know and prepares them should anything I am asking potentially alter how they are calling the show.

Here are some ways I have found to be successful in distributing notes to actors, specifically knowing that getting to an actor before a show can be tricky. I have sent notes via email CCing stage management and explicitly asking actors to reply confirming receipt and understanding. This is my preferred method as it creates a documented trail and a sense of accountability. To create open lines of communication, I also emphasize my availability for further discussion, inviting them to reach out via email, call, or text.

Another way to get notes out, specifically to the ensemble, is by posting them on the callboard. Any time this is done, I require the actors to initial next to their name, which lets me know it has been seen and received. I typically use this method when I am present in the theatre, allowing me to quickly identify and follow-up with individuals who have not yet initialled. If I am not in the building, I will lean on the dance captain to make sure everyone has received and initialled the note. Over time, one also learns which actors consistently arrive well before half-hour, providing an opportunity for face-to-face delivery.

I also frequently use the stage management team to deliver acting notes and the dance captain to deliver choreography notes directly to the actors. By doing so, I ensure that feedback is communicated clearly and through a personal, face-to-face interaction—minimizing misinterpretation and reinforcing accountability. This approach not only strengthens the chain of communication but also cultivates leadership among the production's core team. As an associate you may feel inclined to deliver every note personally, but I've learned that trusting and elevating your team is essential for long-term success. Empowering stage management and the dance captain ensures their voices are heard and valued. This becomes especially critical if, at any point, you need to step away from the production. Knowing the team is already equipped and confident to lead ensures a seamless transition and allows them to lead with confidence.

For complex notes or those requiring the full company, I collaborate with stage management to schedule a rehearsal. Although these demand extra time, they are essential for achieving clarity when dealing with the full company or a note that specifically needs to be addressed on stage. Coming into these sessions with a clear plan and articulating that to the company helps expedite this process and makes sure everyone's time is being used wisely.

There will certainly be times an actor views receiving a note as a judgment of their performance, causing them to become resistant and defensive. When confronted by an actor who is giving you pushback, the most critical resolution in these moments is to remain calm and clear, never allowing the situation to get heated, or for you to display signs of defensiveness. Tension can arise when an actor believes a note contradicts previous direction. This is where meticulous documentation from the rehearsal process becomes your strongest ally. Being able to cross-reference your notes allows you to stand by your direction, knowing you have the source information documented. Whether you

Richard J. Hinds rehearsing the national tour of *Elf*.
Credit: Richard Bowditch

can instantly recall the specific detail or need a moment to confirm and return to the actor, having those details will allow you to give that note with complete confidence.

When facing a "gray area" note—one that lacks specific prior documentation—offering a clear assurance that you will take full and complete responsibility should any other creative question the requested adjustment is helpful. This strategy not only builds trust and demonstrates accountability but also empowers the actor to make the adjustment, knowing you are standing firmly behind them. Ultimately, effective note-giving as an associate is a blend of diplomatic resolve, informed authority, and proactive accountability, fostering a respectful environment.

When approaching a potentially sensitive conversation with an actor, it is essential to consider the setting. I suggest gathering them in a more private environment where they will not be self-conscious about fellow cast members listening in. Stepping into these situations where resistance is anticipated, the strategic presence of a second representative is helpful in protecting yourself. Knowing they are being observed by more than one person can prompt an actor to temper their approach, recognizing that their words and actions are being witnessed and potentially documented. Ideally, this accompanying figure should hold a position of authority, such as a member of stage management, ensuring they possess the gravitas and understanding to effectively intervene if necessary. You never want the actor to feel they are being ganged up upon but having additional support backing you up will hold them accountable and require that the note is received and implemented. Having a witness and an advocate present during these more complex scenarios is not just about safety; it's about establishing an environment that promotes a more constructive resolution.

- ***Voltaire Wade-Green – Associate Choreographer – RAGTIME – Lincoln Center***
  "Ah, everyone's favorite topic . . . notes! Lol. I like to send notes individually by email—clear, concise, and without opinion. I'm always available if someone wants to talk things through.

  Over the years I've had plenty of 'rinse and repeat' note moments, and I've learned that specificity helps everyone. On the day notes go out, I stop by the theatre to check in and make sure things are understood. Sometimes actors take notes personally (I've been there myself!), so I remind them it's all in service of the bigger picture—no need to add pressure to an already intense eight-show week.

  If someone seems resistant, I try to understand their 'why.' Once we connect on that, the tension usually melts, and people are more open to adjustments."
- ***Lauren Stroud – Associate Choreographer – THE WIZARD OF OZ – West End***
  When it comes to delivering notes, I try to be direct and constructive but supportive. I want the actors to feel that they can talk through anything with me, but I also keep the integrity of the original choreography and direction at the forefront of my decisions. My responsibility is to protect what was built in the rehearsal room not to reinvent it. I'm always clear that a note is never personal—it exists purely to strengthen the show as a whole and to make sure the right story is being told.

  If an actor seems defensive or resistant I give them room to share what they're feeling with me. Often just allowing them to voice their opinion helps shift the energy and removes any awkwardness or tension. I gently guide the conversation back to the bigger picture, which should remind them that the note helps elevate the work, keep the company clean, and maintain the vision that the creative team established in the first place. Once we reconnect on that, any tension usually eases and we can move forward together for the good of the show."

Documentation and the Blocking Bible

Documenting and creating a comprehensive Blocking Bible is arguably the single most critical expectation for any associate working on Broadway today. Although various methods exist, the industry standard for charting and blocking is Stage Write. This app was developed by veteran associate Jeff Whiting and helps document and track all the "moving pieces" of a show, such as performer movements, scenery, and props. For those unfamiliar, I'd advise you to immerse yourself in the app as soon as possible, taking advantage of its extensive online tutorials and seeking guidance from experienced users. You will be much better off going into any production already knowing how to use this app rather than trying to learn while on the job.

The app lists the following features on its website . . .

- **DIGITAL SCRIPT**

  Import a PDF of your script and make notes on blocking, traffic, and lighting cues to create your calling script. Taking notes in the white space on your script has never been easier. Plus, you can link your spacing charts to the script, allowing the user to flip back and forth between the chart and the script with ease.

  Enter lighting cues, take down blocking, document choreography, track props. You can even insert a new page, replace a page, allowing you greater ease to create your calling book.

  Link your spacing charts to the section of the script that applies and flip back and forth between the spacing charts and the script so you can see it all at-a-glance.

- **SPACING CHARTS**

  Spacing charts allow the user to document the positions and traffic patterns of actors, scenery, props, and all of the moving parts in a production, by creating snapshot views of every formation and movement of the production in accurate dimension. User easily imports the ground plan for the space, creates icons for each performer, and then creates each chart to track the movement of each piece in the production.

- **COLLABORATION**

  Put everyone on the same page.

  Share your production and collaborate with your team, giving everyone access to edit, view, and share changes in real time.

  Easily share your charts, script, and production with your creative team, giving them access to edit and view work. You can customize what elements you want to share, and which you want to keep private.

- **STAGING SCORE**

  The STAGING SCORE is our patented alternative to using the script to document action and choreography in precise detail.

  Much like a conductor of a symphony can see what each individual instrument is playing at the same time by looking at its Orchestral Score, the Staging Score allows the Stage Write user to see the detail of choreography, blocking, traffic, timing of every moving piece in their production at the same time, and see how it corresponds to the musical counts or lines of dialogue in the production in as much detail as the user desires.

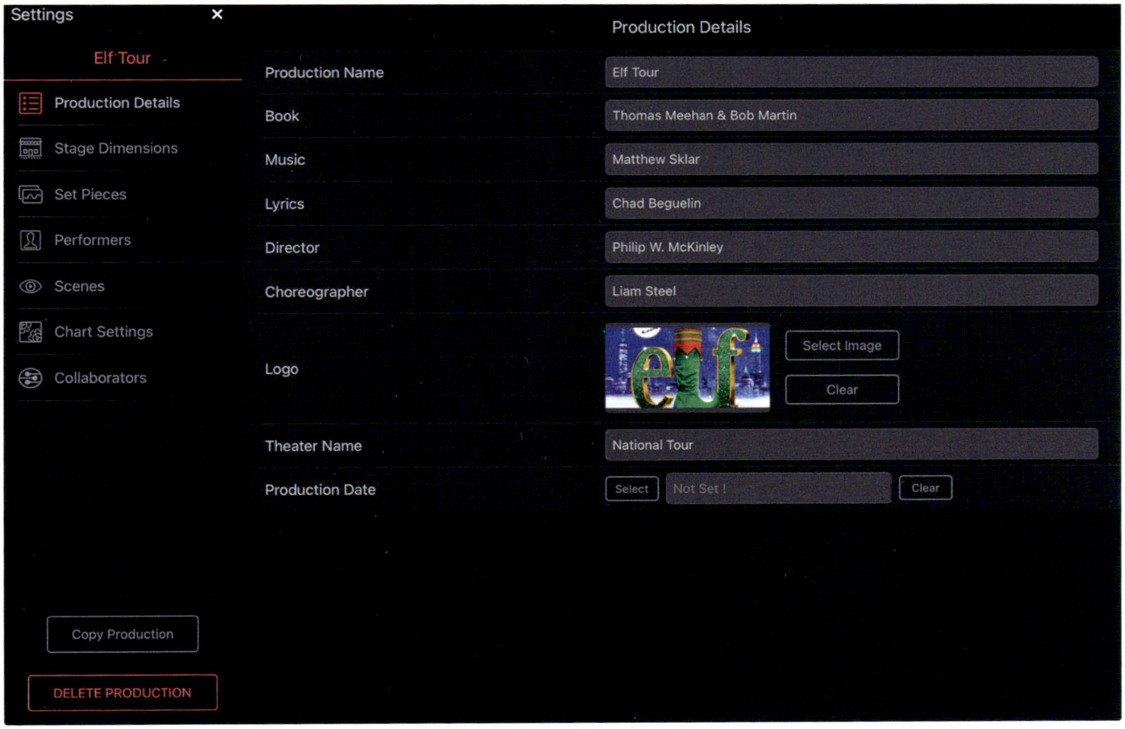

Stage Write setup including Production Details.

Credit: Richard J. Hinds

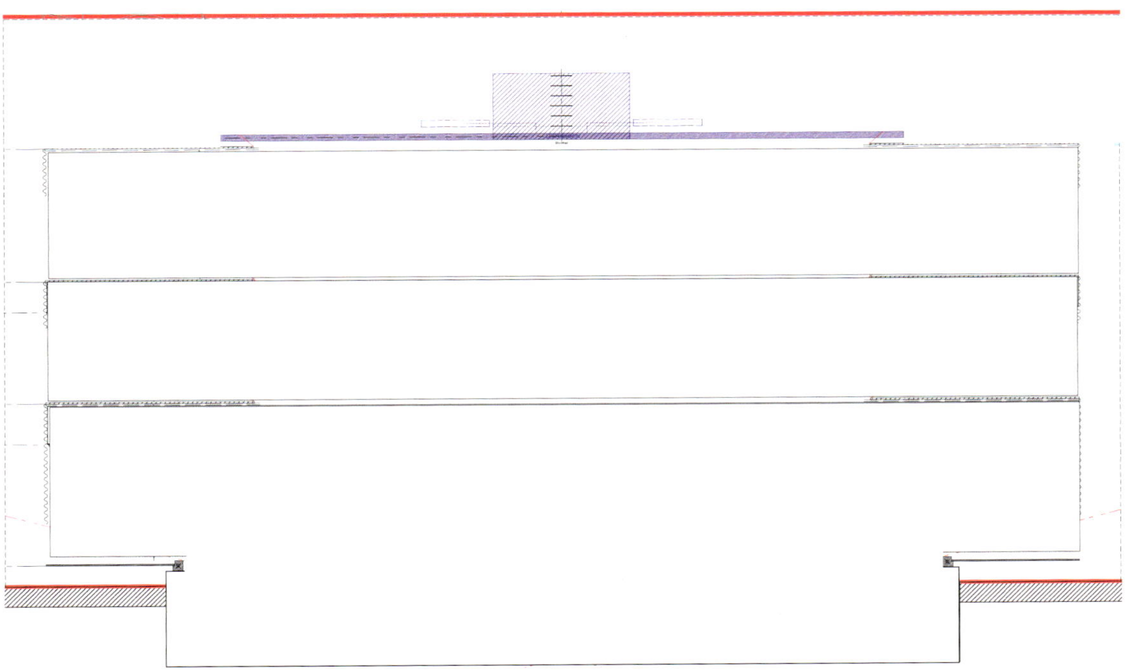

Blank ground plan from *Elf*.

Credit: Richard J. Hinds

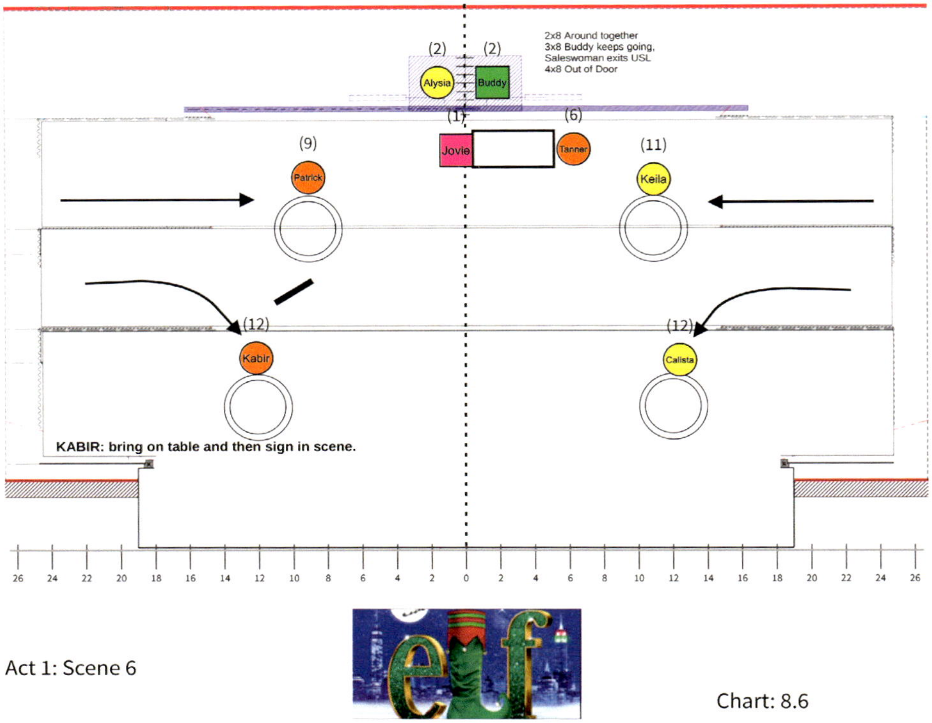

An example of a chart from *Elf* showing entrances into a scene using arrows to show specifically which wing the actors are entering from.

Credit: Richard J. Hinds

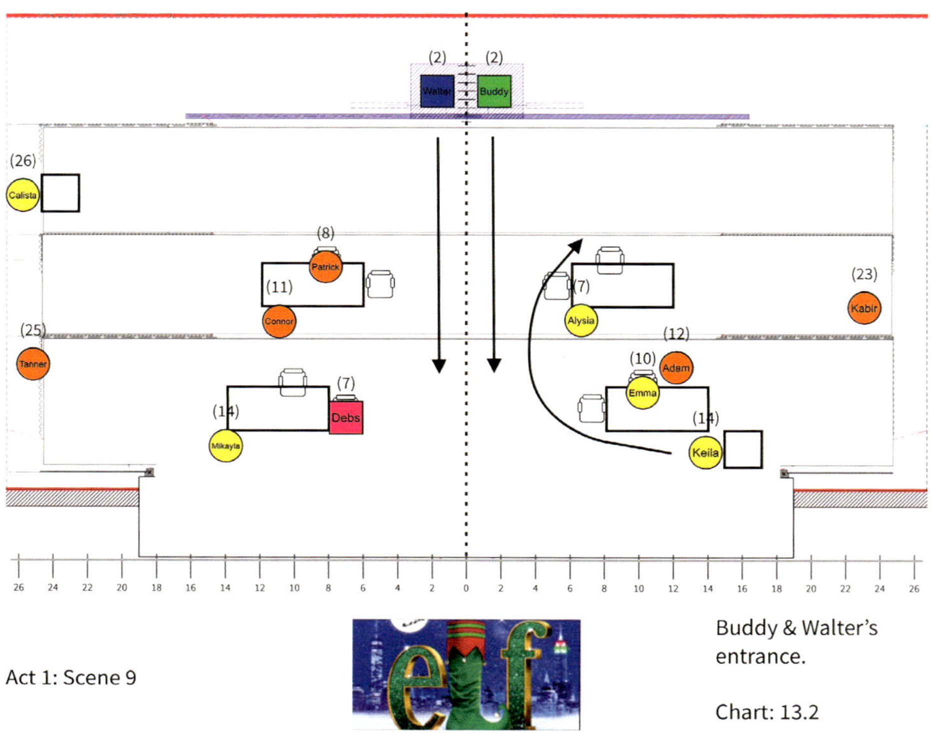

An example of a chart from *Elf* showing how actors enter into a scene as well as internal traffic.

Credit: Richard J. Hinds

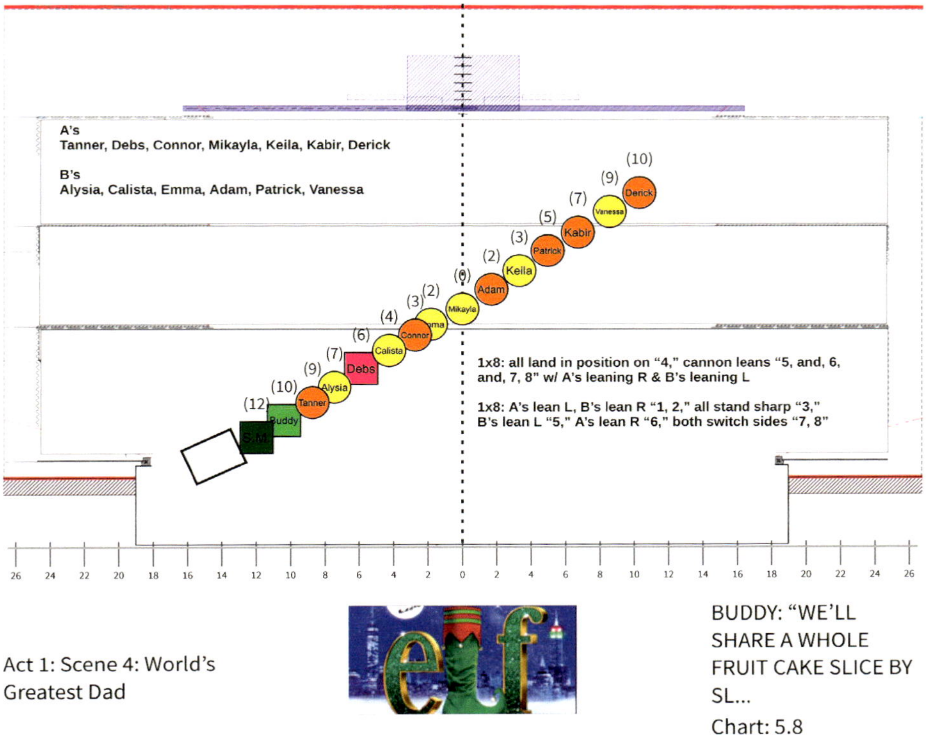

An example of a chart from *Elf* showing a specific formation as well as detailing a specific section of the choreography.

Credit: Richard J. Hinds

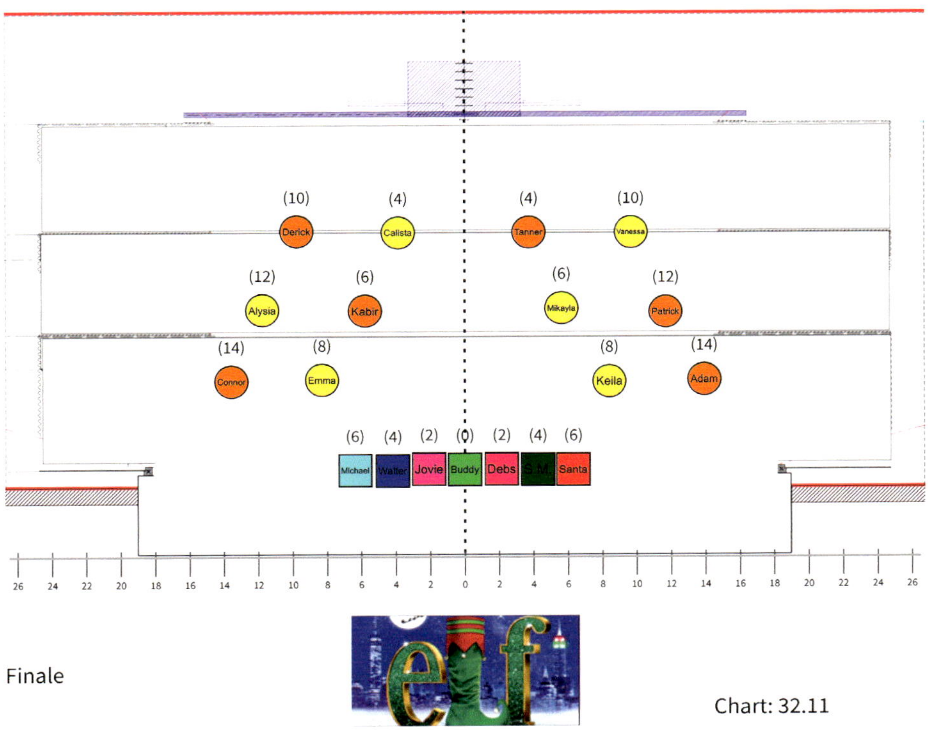

An example of a chart from *Elf* showing a specific formation.

Credit: Richard J. Hinds

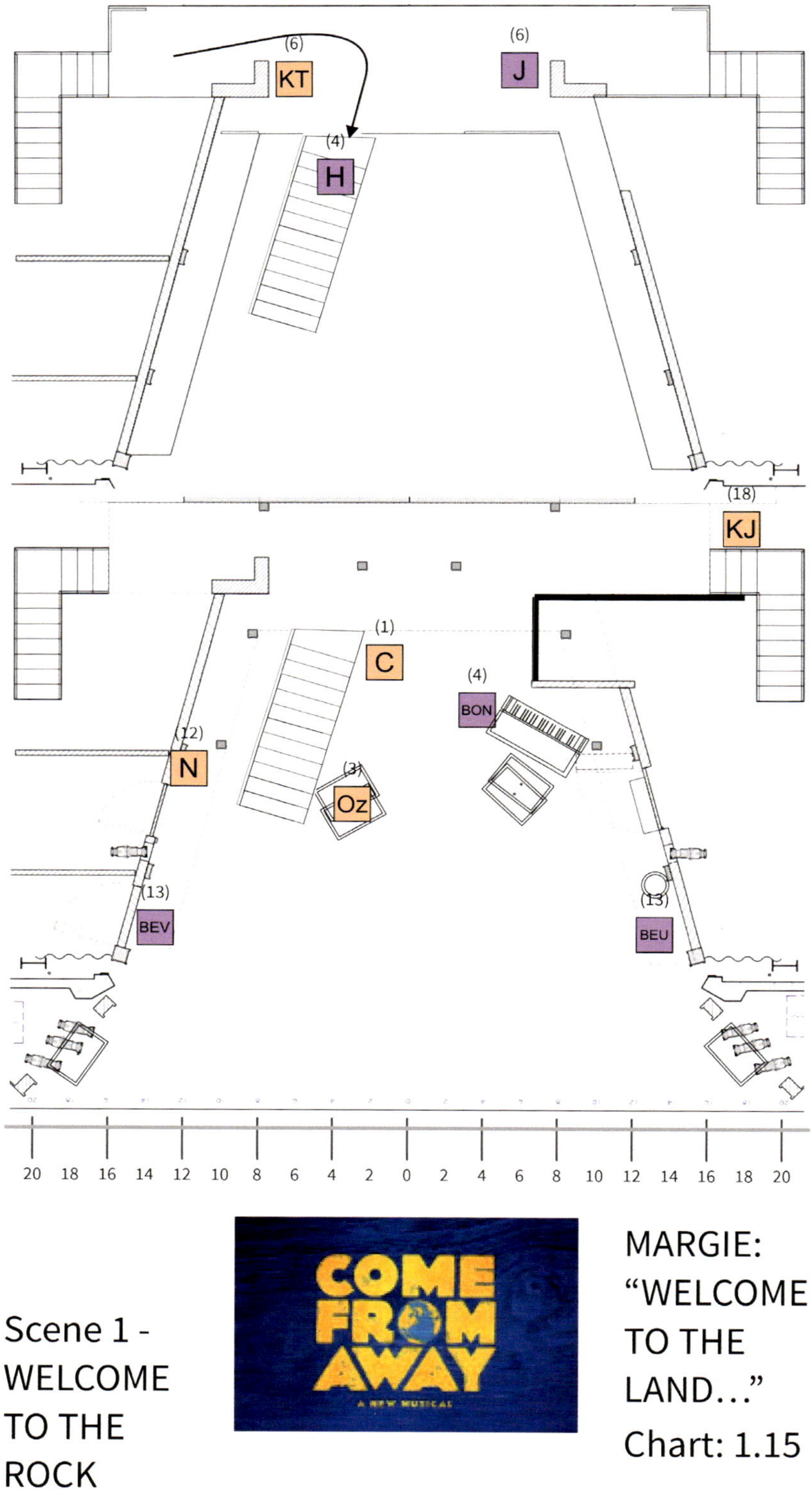

An example of a chart from *Come From Away* demonstrating a two-level set showing blocking downstairs and upstairs.

Credit: Richard J. Hinds

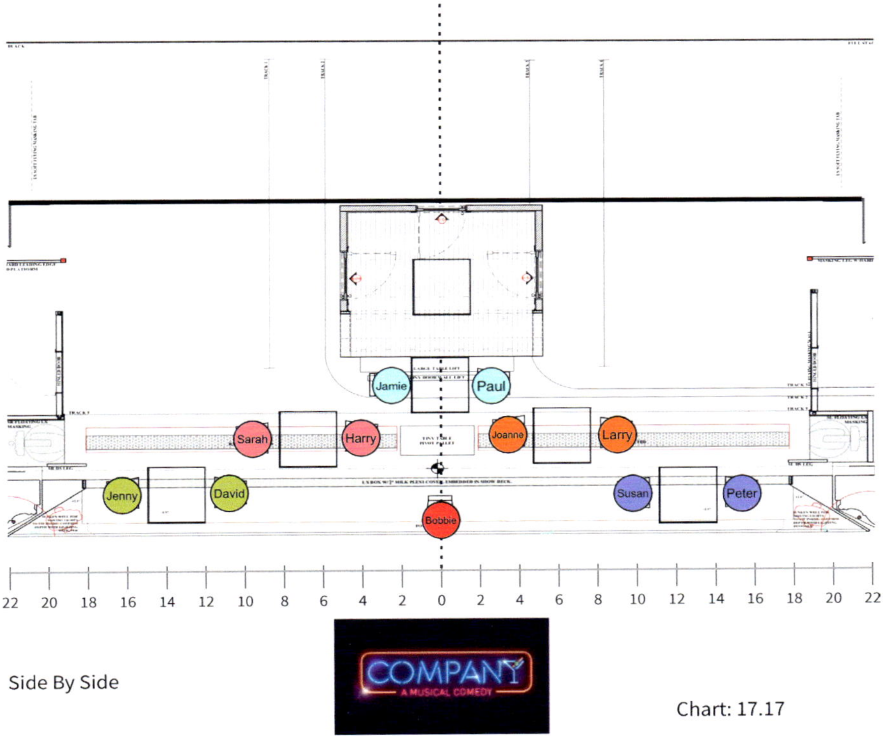

An example of a chart from *Company* showing a specific formation.

Credit: Richard J. Hinds

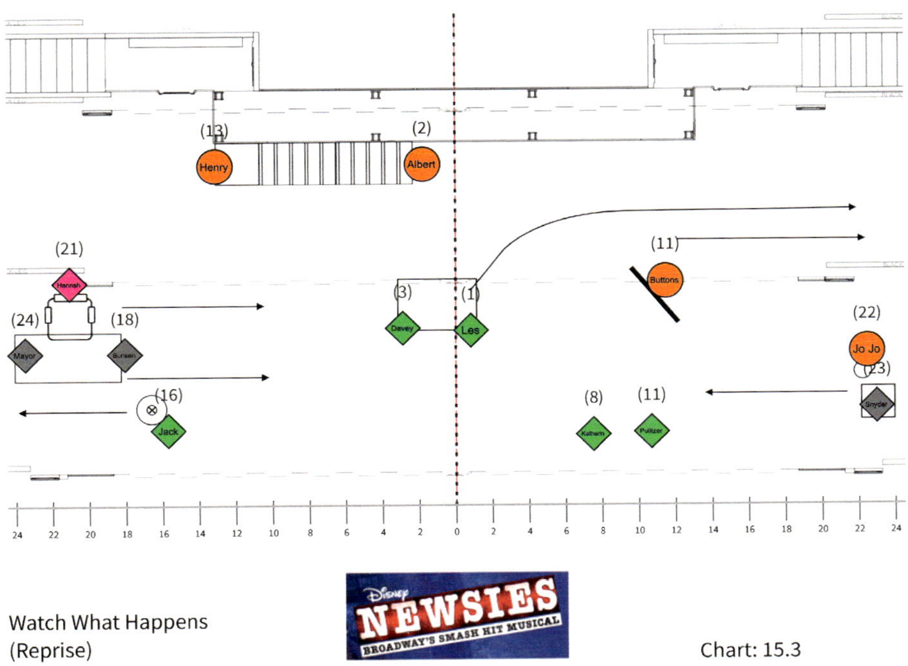

An example of a chart from *Newsies* showing a transition detailing who is taking what scenic pieces on and off.

Credit: Richard J. Hinds

COME FROM AWAY

Scene 1

SONG #1: WELCOME TO THE ROCK

A bodhrán beats a fast rhythm.

ENTRANCES (1x8) ALL start pulsing:

Bonnie (SR1, X to 11SR)
Kevin J (SR1, X to 13SR, DS of Bonnie)
Beverley (SR2, X DS of Table 1 to 3SR by USL corner of Table 1)
Oz (SR2, X to 7SR, US of Bonnie)
Bob (SR2, X to sit on DSL corner of Table 1)
Hannah (SR2, X to 9SR, US of Oz)

Janice (SL1, X to 9SL)
Kevin T (SL1, X to 14SL, sit on DS side of Table 3 facing SR)
Claude (SL2, X to 1SL)
Nick (SL2, X to 4SL in line with Chair 11)
Beulah (SL2, X to 7SL in line w/ US side of Table 2)
Diane (SL2, X to 11SL, just US of Table 3)

11 (CLAUDE) (1SL, SR grey "Janice" spike)
On the northeast tip of North America, on an island called Newfoundland, there's an airport – it used to be one of the biggest airports in the world. And next to it, is a town called Gander. (X US to Table 2)

7 (OZ)
There's a two-person police department. (X US to USR corner of Chair 8)
Nick (X to 2SR US of Oz, behind Chair 7)

4 (BEULAH) (step DS)
An elementary school. (X around Chair 11, end USR of Chair 11)

5 (BONNIE) (X SR)
An SPCA. (X DS of Table 2 to the SL side of Chair 9, 7SL)

An example of a page from the *Come From Away* Blocking Bible that uses an image for reference and also lists all of the blocking embedded into the script.

Credit: Richard J. Hinds

CLAUDE

If you're looking for news, you should talk to that man running in here. That's our constable, Oz Fudge. He's full of stories.

Paul W. (enters from SL1, X DS of Table 2, end 6SR)

OZ (X to 6SR)

Mister mayor, I saw your car in the lot. Crystal, turn up the radio so's we all can hear. Doug, you probably want to get down to Air Traffic Control right away.

Sharon W. (take visor off, put on tree SR)

DOUG (stand and step DS to 3SL)

There's only supposed to be two air traffic controllers on, but instead there's fourteen... Everyone's heard and they all shows up without even being asked. We're told there'll be over 200 planes getting diverted across the **country.** (**ALL** shift after **"country"**)

SHIFT:

Q S. (enter SL1, move Chair 12, stand Chair 12, facing DSR)

De'Lon G. (move Chair 13 on SR side of Rachel T., stand Chair 13, facing DSR)

Rachel T. (move Chair 10 on SL side of De'Lon G., stand Chair 10, facing DSR)

James S. (pull Chair 4 DSR so R front leg is on gray "4" spike, stand Chair 3, facing DSR)

Sharon W. (stand Chair 4, facing DSL)

Paul W. (stand Chair 5, take hat off, facing DSL)

Astrid V. (stand Chair 6, facing DSL)

Joel H. (stand Chair 7, facing DSL)

Caesar S. (stand Chair 8, facing DSR)

Jim W. (stand Chair 9, facing DSR)

Petrina B. (stand Chair 11, facing DSL)

Emily W. (exit SR2 US of Table 1, put on Flight Attendant)

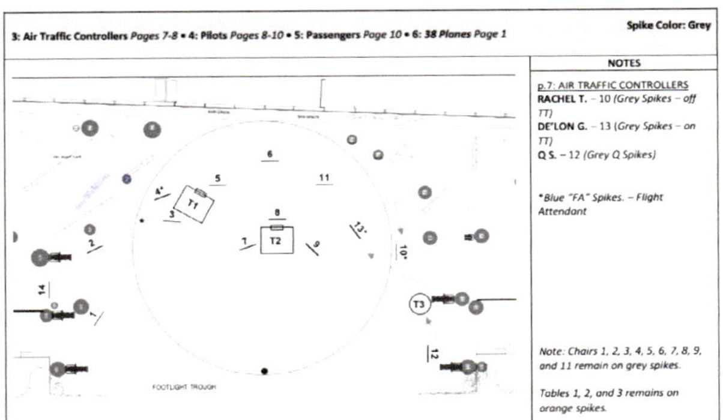

An example of a page from the *Come From Away* Blocking Bible that uses an image for reference, has a Stage Write chart for reference, and also lists all of the blocking embedded into the script.

Credit: Richard J. Hinds

Sharon W. (end splitting Chairs 2 & 3)
Jim W. (end splitting Chairs 10 & 11)

DIANE & NICK

TAKE A PICTURE OF THE SCENERY
OF A LOOKOUT
OF A MOMENT WHICH IS OVER
OF THE OCEAN OF THE RIVER OF THE **TREES** (turntable stops)

Sharon W. (look to Jim W. on "**TREES**")
Jim W. (look to Sharon W. on cutoff of "**TREES**")
Sharon W., Jim W. (both look front)

FORMATION:

James S. (11SR, splitting Pink "Beverley" spike)
Rachel T. (10SR, R foot on "Purple T2" spike)
Q S. (8SR, R foot on US "Pink 10" spike)
Joel H. (4SR, L foot on "Red/Brown 13" spike)
De'Lon G. (3SR, R foot on "Yellow Jim" spike)
Petrina B. (1SR, US of Table 2)

Astrid V. (2SL, in between Table 1 & 2)
Paul W. (4SL, R foot on "Brown 8" spike)
Caesar S. (5SL, L foot on "Gray 3" spike)
Emily W. (X btwn Caesar S. and Astrid V. to 8SL, R foot on "Blue Bob" spike)

DIANE & NICK

STOP THE WORLD **PLEASE** (**Joel H.** X DS to 10SR)

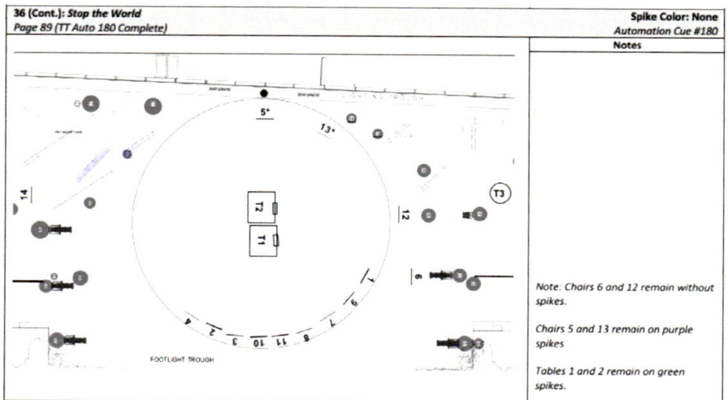

An example of a page from the *Come From Away* Blocking Bible that uses an image for reference, has a Stage Write chart for reference, and also lists all of the blocking embedded into the script.

Credit: Richard J. Hinds

- **IPAD APP**

  The Stage Write iPad App is FREE and allows you to access and edit your data on the go! Simply log into your account on the iPad.

  The FREE app allows you to edit spacing charts, mark your script, document choreography and staging, and sync the data between devices and between members of your team!

  The iPad app also works in offline mode so you can take the iPad into the theatre—even if there's no internet—you can continue your work and when you return to internet, sync the data to the web and share with your collaborators.

Although Stage Write initially requires a dedicated learning curve, once you are familiar with the app it becomes an indispensable tool for efficiently capturing the staging of a production. The process begins with meticulous setup, starting with standard "production details" (production name, book, music, lyrics, director, choreographer, logo, theatre name, production date) before defining the most important information—the dimensions of the stage—which are then locked-in for the entire production, allowing for it to be shown in scale. This step requires you to know the dimension of the space or, if importing a ground plan, measuring at least one dimension of the imported ground plan. Typically received from the production manager or set designer, the ground plan is usually stripped from all technical specifics, such as lineset schedules or sightlines, to focus specifically on the stage itself, the entrances and exits, and any defining features such as tracks or elevators. Once the physical space is defined, you add performers (labelled with different shapes and colors), scenes, and songs. There are other actions available but the initial ones I have listed are the essential ones.

Now, the charting begins. You will start by adding a blank chart (the initial ground plan you uploaded) and from there you can add which performers are in the scene or song and where they are located. For more detail, you can add set pieces and scenic elements as well, so the chart is an exact replica of what is seen on stage. As you start dictating formation shifts and specific blocking, there is a collection of shapes (arrows, circles, squares, etc.) that you can input to help make these patterns clear. You also have the ability to add a text box into any chart if you wish to include specific detail regarding traffic patterns, a prop pass off, or a musical timing. There is a designated box on the bottom of each chart where you can include text specifying the exact cue line or lyric that initiates the action, guaranteeing absolute clarity.

This documentation part of the process can be overwhelming and time-consuming, which is why initiating this charting process during the pre-production period is crucial for cutting down on the workload once rehearsals commence. Although you won't necessarily have all the specifics during these early stages, the foundation will be there, allowing the rehearsal period to be about adding critical specifics: noting precise entrances and exits, marking where set pieces land on the floor, and mapping intricate traffic patterns. When deciding how much is too much, adopt the mindset that the chart is being built for someone completely unfamiliar with the show; the greater the specificity, the clearer it will be. Often you are not just making this for yourself, but for the longevity of the production, and it will become a tool for other people to use as well including stage management and dance captains. Using the assistance of your dance captain can be very helpful to cross-reference numbers, depths, and traffic patterns, ensuring the information is as accurate as possible. Having multiple eyes verifying the documentation significantly reduces the possibility of incorrect information being recorded.

The Blocking Bible functions as the ultimate detailed counterpart to standard Stage Write charts, creating a script-integrated resource essential for documenting the show. This document is meticulously constructed by embedding all specific stage directions—including actor entrances and exits, what props they have, what costumes pieces they are wearing, etc.—directly into the script, effectively marrying the physical blocking to the text itself. To keep the entire team "on the same page," literally, the Blocking Bible is formatted to mirror the script's pagination, often utilizing the adjacent blank page for comprehensive notes. Because of the significant time commitment required for this level of detail, the sooner you start this, the better. I typical write everything down during the rehearsal process in chicken scratch and then go home at night, clean up my notes, and then carefully integrate them into the script. Once combined with the Stage Write documentation, this master bible becomes a comprehensive resource.

For those bringing in residents and local associates while mounting multiple companies, these detailed records transform into invaluable learning tools, enabling them to come to rehearsals thoroughly prepared. For *Come From Away* specifically, this documentation proved to be a critical tool. I would provide local residents with this material, alongside an archival video, allowing them to familiarize themselves with the show's nuances long before rehearsals commenced. Furthermore, these resources empowered them to maintain the show with accuracy and allowed them to have true ownership of their title once they were left to manage the show themselves.

As *Come From Away* was being prepared to be licensed, I was commissioned to create a definitive staging bible. This document was intended to serve as a guide for creative teams worldwide, many of whom would have minimal knowledge of the original production, to better understand the show. Given the fast paced, incredibly intricate nature of the staging, this bible demanded extensive detail, documenting every single piece of blocking, prop exchange, and costume piece add-on to successfully mount the production. To make sure I had captured the required level of specificity, I submitted early drafts to a select group of trusted fellow associates, asking "*Using only this document, could you confidently stage the show*"? Their feedback was key, highlighting areas that needed more detail. Because the creation of this bible was exclusively for the licensing entity, Music Theatre International, I was compensated for my work, making this the first time I had earned a fee specifically for creating this kind of bible.

- ***Voltaire Wade-Green – Associate Choreographer – RAGTIME – Lincoln Center***

  "Google Docs and Stage Write are my lifesavers—I love them both!

  Google Docs lets me keep a live working document and collaborate with others in real time, which is especially helpful when multiple people are noting at once.

  Stage Write is my go-to for tracking. It can be a bit tedious on larger shows, but it's incredibly useful and saves so much time when mapping out where everyone goes."

- ***Lauren Stroud – Associate Choreographer – THE WIZARD OF OZ – West End***

  I use a combination of Stage Write, Nebo, and Google Docs/Word to keep the entire production organized and consistent. Stage Write is my main hub—all spacing charts, maps, diagrams and consolidated tracking eventually end up there. But during rehearsals I rely heavily on an app called Nebo. It's like an endless digital notepad on my iPad, which is perfect for quickly sketching maps and jotting down thoughts in the moment when listening to the choreographer set a number. Once the rehearsal day is over or things feel more settled in tech, I will then transfer those notes into Stage Write so everything is clean and fully documented.

For covers and swings I create spreadsheets, cheat sheets, and tables in Google Docs or Word. These help me track the most crucial elements of each person's track—especially the moments that can't be cut if we're running a show with fewer people. Each tool serves a different purpose and when used together they give me a clear, reliable system that supports the show from every angle.

Tech

Moving into the theatre is a thrilling moment in any production's process. It's the culmination of months of work where all the departments are together under one roof seeing their vision come to life on stage for the first time.

Once you have entered the theatre and made your way into the house, you'll find preassigned tech tables thoughtfully arranged and clearly labelled, making it easy to identify each department and its designated space. Familiarizing yourself quickly with this layout will be a valuable asset allowing you to navigate efficiently between each department. Moving into the theatre brings many new faces, and taking the opportunity to introduce yourself and get to know your colleagues can

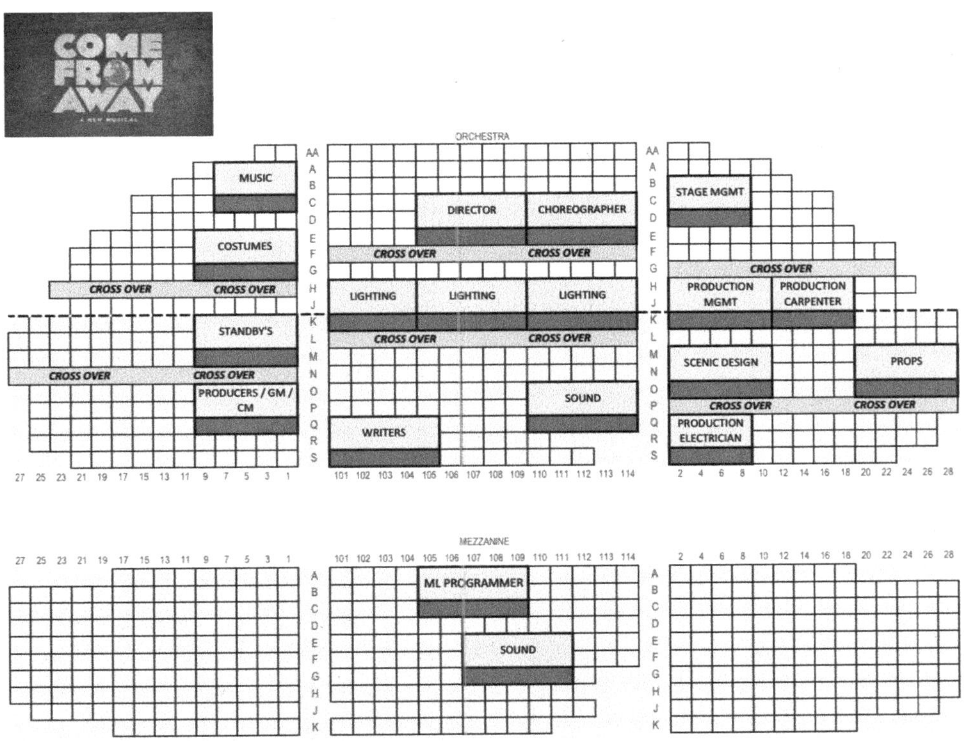

Tech table setup for *Come From Away* on Broadway.

Credit: Guy Kwan: Juniper Street Productions, Inc.

go a long way in building a supportive environment. By now, most designers are accompanied by their associates, who will soon become key points of contact. These associates will frequently interact with you, sharing vital information, cross-referencing paperwork, and seeking your knowledge when needed—making strong, clear communication essential.

Once I have met the team out front, I go backstage and introduce myself to the crew and learn everyone's name; from flymen, to dressers, to automation . . . EVERYONE! You'd be surprised how many crew members I have had come up to me and thank me for addressing them by their name and telling me how often that does not happen. These are the individuals who will be instrumental in making sure the show runs smoothly and are just as much part of the team as anyone else. Their willingness to contribute and problem-solve is directly linked to feeling seen and valued and the simple act of addressing them by name will do just that.

After you have settled into your station at your tech table next to your creative team, the craziness of tech truly begins. One of the first things to happen is "dry tech," a technical rehearsal without actors to rehearse non-performance elements of a show, such as scenic changes, projections, lighting cues, and sound effects. During these rehearsals, an associate will usually be on stage standing in for the actors. It is imperative to have every actor's blocking notated and easily accessible, allowing you to step in for anyone with precision and clarity. You may be asked to stand in an actor's spot where they are singing a solo for a light to be focused on you. You may be asked to walk an actor's traffic pattern for scenic elements to be cued around you. You being able to execute these requests with clarity will prevent the team from having to dissect these moments later during full tech.

Tech rehearsals for the national tour of *Jekyll & Hyde*.

Credit: Billy Bustamante

These dry tech sessions often present unforeseen challenges, as this is the first time the creative team is interacting with the design fully completed: a set piece is larger than anticipated, sight lines require an actor to move downstage to be seen, or an entrance changes because a set piece is blocking the wing. When these modifications occur, it becomes your responsibility to take scrupulous notes—documenting every shift, every new mark, every altered traffic pattern—and pass these changes onto the actors, usually verbally so they can ask any questions they have but also by typing them up and distributing them so they have a hard copy to reference later.

Once you move into full tech and the actors join you, an associate will become the liaison, bridging the gap between the creatives in the house and the actors onstage. You will be running back and forth from the tech tables to being on stage, guaranteeing you will get your steps for the day. You should always try to be problem-solving, anticipating and addressing challenges before they even come up, in an attempt to keep the tech session moving at a steady pace. The transition from the rehearsal room to the stage, integrating sets, lights, sound, and costumes, will inevitably present unforeseen shifts in blocking, spacing, and traffic. Since you will often be moving on and offstage, not always with your notes, your dance captain will prove to be very helpful making sure all charts and blocking are being updated in real-time and will serve as your eyes and ears. Whenever you have a moment, connect with them to cross-reference your notes against theirs to make sure nothing has been overlooked.

When a particular transition isn't working as planned, an associate is able to provide an extra set of eyes on stage. Although the creative team will likely continue to observe from the audience to provide a front-of-house perspective, an associate often stays onstage helping to solve the problem. Stage management will also be very helpful in these situations, although their perspective tends to be specifically through a technical lens, whereas an associate is looking at it through a more artistic one. Having a first-hand account of what is going on allows an associate to clearly articulate to the creative team what is happening and potentially offer a solution.

Your director or choreographer will be filtering technical notes to you throughout the tech process, which you'll be responsible for meticulously organizing by department. This organization will prove to be helpful for the end-of-day production meeting, where the entire creative team comes together to check in and share notes. To help cut down on these meeting times, you may be asked to deliver notes to specific departments throughout the day. This not only helps to streamline the production meeting but also allows the designers to get a head start on what's being asked of them.

During the whirlwind of a tech process, staying organized is critical. The days are long and having a great system of notetaking will make sure nothing slips through the cracks. The key lies in effectively documenting every piece of information that is being given to you so that at the end of the day you can look back over your notes and understand exactly what they mean. You will then be able to articulate this exact information to your director or choreographer in a clear and concise manner. As lists grow and tasks accumulate, attempting to check things off throughout the day will help you from feeling overwhelmed. Organization serves as the essential foundation for a smooth, successful tech process, turning chaos into cohesion and laying the groundwork for a polished final product.

Previews to Opening Night

The preview period is considered to be the single most educational phase of any production. During this crucial stage, the missing ingredient—the audience—is finally added, providing the creative team with invaluable information before the show is officially "frozen," meaning all technical and physical changes must stop. The audience will provide the creative team with invaluable feedback through their reactions and engagement. A punchline might receive a chuckle instead of uproarious laughter, a dance sequence might outstay its welcome, or a nuanced relationship might require further development to truly connect with the audience. However, this period must be handled carefully. It's tempting to react instantaneously to every perceived flaw, but one must resist the urge to jump to conclusions. One night you might have a subdued audience, while the very next performance will generate rock-concert-like responses. Therefore, navigating the preview period requires that the adjustments being made are being done so judiciously guaranteeing that the changes being made are not impulsive, but strategic.

During preview performances, an associate will be sat beside their director or choreographer to write down every whispered note, while also taking their own notes of anything they see that a creative might have missed. During intermission and as soon as the curtain falls, the real sprint begins. As you are not able to have your laptop open during the performance, notes are usually scribbled down on paper in the dark and then typed up both at intermission and at the end of the show. You must swiftly organize these scattered notes into a clear, legible, and logically structured document, separating your actor notes from your tech notes. This must then be printed and delivered to the creative with efficiency, often within minutes. Speed is non-negotiable; the director or choreographer will need these notes before meeting with the actors for notes or the creative team for a production meeting. Since you will likely be running around until these tasks are completed, make sure you are always accessible to your creative, usually by phone, should they need to get a hold of you during this window.

Following each preview performance, the producers and creative team, associates included, will once again gather for a production meeting. However, this time, this post-show debrief will include discussing what was learned from watching the show that evening and identifying areas for improvement. This meeting concludes with the stage management team, or associates, creating a detailed **work list**, charting a precise course of action for the next day's intensive four-to-five-hour rehearsal block. This list will often include the page number in question, the scene and/or song, the actors involved, what the change is, and a cue line to ensure everyone begins precisely at the right place. To maximize efficiency, time allocations for each moment being addressed are often included to help keep the team on track and ensure the rehearsal process runs as smoothly as possible.

The ripple effect of a single change can be profound. Cutting a scene, for instance, will require connecting one moment to the next, which previously had not happened. This will include reconfiguring set transitions, potentially creating new quick changes for actors, altering transition music, and redesigning lighting cues. Every department, from stage management to technical crews, will feel the impact. An associate will often be asked to generate a list of the exact ramifications a large adjustment might create and will use their expertise to help problem solve. In moments like this, referencing your documentation to gather the modifications that need to be made for this change to work will help streamline problem-solving.

Once the afternoon rehearsal is complete, an associate assumes responsibility for compiling the change log. This document functions much as it did during tech, with one key difference: the limited time to distribute it. The window between the end of rehearsal and half-hour can be tight, requiring efficiency. Updating the document throughout rehearsal helps expedite the process and ensures it reaches the cast as quickly as possible.

WORK LIST (1pm - 5pm)

PAGE #	SCENE/SONG	ACTOR	NOTE	TIME
Pg. 20	***LOOK AT ME, I'M SANDRA DEE*** Cue: RIZZO: *"Let's hope she stays out. She is really boring."*	Rizzo, Marty, Frenchy	Re-stage choreography around bed so that Rizzo stays further DS on the edge of bed and Marty and Frenchie stay sitting on the sides	1pm - 1:30pm
Pg. 23	***GREASED LIGHTNING*** Cue: KENICKIE: *"Why it's "Greased Lightning"!"*	Kenickie, Danny, Roger, Sonny, Male Ensemble	Need to light the start of the song so the T-Birds are more bright and there is less light on the Male Ensemble	1:30pm - 2pm
BREAK				2pm - 2:10pm
Pg. 23	***GREASED LIGHTNING*** Cue: KENICKIE: *"Why it's "Greased Lightning"!"*	Kenickie, Danny, Roger, Sonny, Male Ensemble	Add more strobe lights when the Male Ensemble start clapping around the car. Need a more "rock concert" look here	2:10pm - 2:30pm
Pg. 26	***Act 1, Scene 7*** Cue: SANDY: *"Do a split, give a yell…"*	Sandy, Danny, Patty	Need to re-spike the bleachers so they are further DS. This means looking at the blocking in the scene to make sure it works and also checking the lighting	2:30pm - 3pm
BREAK				3pm - 3:10pm
Pg. 37	***BORN TO HAND JIVE*** Cue: VINCE: *"AWAY WE GO!"*	Full Company	1) Clean the first dance break and check the spacing of the couples 2) Add more light around Vince when he runs into Marty 3) Clean Miss Lynch's traffic pattern walking through the couples 4) Check last pose to make sure everyone is lit	3:10pm - 5pm

An example of a "work list".
Credit: Richard J. Hinds

A core function of an associate during the preview period is the preparation of the show's understudies, or "covers." The role of an essential offstage cover involves them being present from day one of rehearsals, diligently observing and absorbing as much as possible, often from their designated station or on the sides. Although this observational learning is vital, it presents a very different experience from the onstage company who are actively rehearsing in the correct space, interacting with props, and learning alongside the full cast. Sometimes it will become even more complicated when an onstage actor has an understudy assignment requiring them to simultaneously learn their own show, as well as their cover's. For the understudies, on and offstage, their comprehensive "put-in" rehearsal—the full run-through incorporating the entire onstage company and all technical elements—is typically put off until after the official opening. Consequently, a vulnerability exists: understudies may be called upon to perform during the preview process without ever having truly rehearsed their tracks with the full cast, orchestra, and technical elements.

Most of the Broadway productions I've worked on have seen a cover step into a role well before opening night. When that inevitable, panicked last-minute call comes, it is typically the associate who steps up to make sure the cover is fully prepped and confident to step on stage that night in front of an audience. This will include walking them through every nuance of their track, making sure every piece of choreography is executed precisely, every scene is approached with the appropriate emotional and dramatic intentions, and that every entrance and exit is made through the correct wing, following exact traffic patterns. Safety always comes first; I make it my absolute priority that covers have a clear understanding of what's happening on stage at all times. They must know the precise placement of every scenic element and navigate every transition, particularly those involving moving

Richard J. Hinds at the Opening Night of *Elf* on Broadway.
Credit: Keven Quillon

Richard J. Hinds and Liam Steel at the Opening Night of *Elf* in the West End.

Credit: Richard J. Hinds

Richard J. Hinds and Kelly Devine at the Opening Night of *Come From Away* in Toronto.

Credit: Richard J. Hinds

scenery or challenging dark lighting cues. Although the director and choreographer have ultimately crafted and built the show, they don't necessarily always know all the intricacies that an associate does—the exact location where an actor puts a prop on stage, the precise traffic internal to a scene, or the specific wing an actor enters from. This is the moment when all those meticulously detailed charts and the comprehensive Blocking Bible truly prove their value.

The preview period, whether a few days or several weeks, is often the most challenging and exhausting period throughout the whole process. It tends to be the longest days an associate puts in throughout the whole contract. Not knowing exactly what changes are coming down the pipeline or what cover might be going on last minute, the preview window can be quite unpredictable. This is the ultimate fight to the finish line. All those months of prep, auditions, rehearsals, tech, and previews all culminate to the thrilling opening night!

Although opening night is intended to be a celebration, as an associate your work is not yet done. Before you can walk the red carpet and soak up the excitement of the evening, there is still work to be done. A list of responsibilities might include distributing opening night gifts, running a last-minute clean-up rehearsal, and, crucially, ensuring that the very last set of actor and production notes have been meticulously distributed. It's important to remember that, while the day is full of celebration, your role is to help keep the company grounded and focused despite the potential chaos and distraction. Most importantly, you *must* be there for your director or choreographer to offer any support they need. This can include picking up their opening night tickets, making sure they are getting where they need to be for different interviews and photo opportunities at the right time, or holding onto any cards or gifts that might be given to them throughout the night. In these final hours, your support and calm presence will help your creative enter into the theatre feeling protected and supported.

An associate, like everyone involved in the production, must prepare themselves for what is to come after the curtain falls. The reviews begin rolling out putting all involved into a make-or-break moment: being the toast of the town or the recipient of harsh critiques. Although one always hopes their show will be embraced, art is subjective, and the critics will make their opinion clearly known. There's very little an associate can do at this point, however, it's important to recognize the impact this specific moment will have and how it will ultimately shape the show's future, which will most definitely affect you.

Maintenance

The expectations of an associate once a show has opened are highly unpredictable until a show's success is determined. For productions categorized as "a hit," the role of the associate expands exponentially to that of a leading role, with you inheriting key maintenance duties, such as leading daily rehearsals, preparing press events, teaching new understudies and replacements, and ensuring artistic integrity. These responsibilities previously fell upon the stage manager or dance captain post-opening but more and more, these are inherited by the associate. In effect, they begin to embody the functions of a "Resident Director" or "Resident Choreographer," a prevalent and highly defined role established in the West End system. Key responsibilities for a resident include:

- **Maintaining artistic standards**: Ensuring that every performance continues to meet the original artistic and creative vision of the director and choreographer.
- **Rehearsing the cast**: Leading rehearsals for understudies, swings, and new cast members, to teach them their roles and integrate them into the production. Also holding occasional brush up rehearsals with the onstage cast.
- **Providing notes**: Watching performances regularly (often several times a week) and providing notes to the company to maintain quality and consistency.
- **Liaising**: Serving as a crucial communication link between the cast, stage management, production management, and the original creative team. This will include checking in with the cast, as well as all other departments, daily.
- **Scheduling**: Working with stage management and company management to schedule rehearsals.
- **Assisting with casting**: Being involved in the re-casting process for new company members.
- **Problem solving**: Being present in the theatre and available to manage any unexpected artistic or personnel issues that arise on short notice.

Although the formal title of "resident" is still inconsistently applied across Broadway contracts, the responsibilities of associates have shifted to meet these standards, requiring their presence in the day-to-day operations of a long-running show.

The immediate, overwhelming critical success of *Come From Away* on Broadway prompted the producers to quickly expand the coverage of the company. This decision involved adding two additional standbys, bringing the count from four to six, beginning a period of intense rehearsal overseen by myself and the Associate Director. We were responsible for preparing these new actors as quickly and thoroughly as possible, using studio rehearsals combined with crucial on-stage time—the turntable being a vital component for mastering the show's blocking. The culmination of this process was the "put-in" rehearsal: a full-scale run through involving the two new standbys in their primary roles, supported by the remaining standbys and main on-stage cast to form a complete company of twelve. These put-ins were executed with full technical support and with the band, allowing the actors to experience the show as close to show conditions as possible. This highly time-consuming and expensive process was repeated until all standbys had been put in for every track they covered.

This system was central to the producers' and creative team's adamant stance that the show's original vision be perfectly maintained. Consequently, I worked in a near full-time capacity to achieve this while also observing the performance several times a week to pass along notes and ensure every detail remained intact. Should any conflicts come up taking me away from the show, it was our exceptional dance captain, Josh Breckenridge, who would step in to continue running the operation when necessary. When possible, I tried to avoid this situation to allow Josh to be present in the track he himself was rehearsing and prevent him from having to wear two hats at once.

The close-knit relationship between an Associate Choreographer and their dance captain is very important. Because the dance captain is there every day, they will have more detailed insight to what is happening in the building on a regular basis. They become your eyes and ears in your absence. They are also very valuable in bringing knowledge to a situation that an associate might not have, since they have experienced the show onstage and can offer a different perspective. It is the dance captain who will step up to handle any situation requiring an immediate response should you not be there.

Although my initial contract concluded on opening night of *Come From Away*, the transition into this non-stop maintenance and leadership role helped when negotiating a new weekly salary. What was being asked of me now was very different from my initial contract as the "Associate Choreographer," putting me in a good position to make sure I was being compensated appropriately.

My journey on *Jekyll & Hyde* was very different. From the beginning, this show operated on a very tight budget. We rehearsed in New York City followed by a six-month national tour designed to build momentum before arriving on Broadway. During its time on the road, I was only requested to check in on the production once, a direct consequence of the producers being highly conscious about conserving the show's budget. When we arrived on Broadway, the opening was met with lukewarm critical praise, and it was immediately clear the show was in trouble. The finances had to be reined in as tightly as possible, which meant I would not be asked to do any day-to-day maintenance, leaving the stage manager and dance captain to expertly run the building. Despite these drastic cost-saving measures, the revival was unable to gain traction, closing after a brief run of fifteen previews and thirty performances on Broadway.

Post-opening, an associate's position is often the first to be cut if a show encounters financial trouble. Heading into this period of limbo is perhaps the most daunting challenge, with an associate typically waiting in the dark, unable to confidently plan the next move until the reviews have come out. There is an unspoken industry expectation to remain indefinitely available, placing your career on a temporary hold. Through experience, however, I have learned to negotiate this uncertainty by prioritizing transparent communication. If I have another project on the horizon, the entire creative and producing team is made aware of my availability limits well in advance, guaranteeing there is a contingency plan in place—whether the dance captain assumes my responsibilities in my absence or a new associate is brought in. Learning to manage expectations between contract completion and a potential extension on your contract is vital. This window can often be filled with anxiety but planning accordingly will help ease this.

Working as an associate on a touring production offers a much more flexible schedule, letting you pursue other opportunities while still being able to fulfill your role. These situations are ideal as it allows you to dictate your availability more specifically. Once a show is up and running, an associate will make visits anywhere from once a month to once every couple of months. Each visit typically involves traveling to the tour's current location, observing a performance to note, and then leading a clean-up rehearsal to ensure the show maintains its original integrity. The duration of these visits can vary from a swift forty-eight-hour in-and-out trip to a full week-long stay, often dictated by the week's overall schedule. During my time with *Come From Away*, my visits would often be booked several months in advance. This allowed stage management to plan rehearsals and ensure the necessary cast and crew were available, while also giving company management ample time to arrange my travel and housing needs. Recognizing the demands placed on a touring company, both the producing team and I always aimed to keep these visits to a minimum. When I would check-in, I would make sure the rehearsal sessions were incredibly productive and efficient so the cast never felt their time was being wasted. This was also a great opportunity for the cast to speak to me directly if there were any moments they felt might have shifted since opening and needed some attention.

Whether working on a Broadway show or a national tour, the associate becomes the face of the creative team once the show is open. Live theatre is a living, breathing organism where things will inevitably evolve and grow. An associate must create an environment where actors feel there is room to breathe while never straying from the production's original vision. Associates will be faced with complicated situations where actors come with notes and opinions regarding another actor's performance and how it is affecting them directly. A critical part of your role is ensuring every individual in the building feels heard, creating a safe space for communication. You then decide the most appropriate next steps, always with the show's integrity and the company's well-being in mind. Ultimately, the associate's ability to navigate these situations, holding the creative vision firm while nurturing growth and discovery, are essential tools to creating a positive environment in the workplace.

When putting a new actor into a role, it is important you communicate with the creative team as to what the parameters are. Different shows have varying expectations regarding an actor's freedom to interpret and deviate from the original blocking. A scene may feature a complex lighting sequence that requires precise timing from the actor, whereas another scene with a simpler lighting setup may offer more freedom for them to move around. Regardless of the approach, it is essential to find a balance that empowers the new actor to take ownership of the role, rather than being made to feel they are a carbon copy of someone else. To achieve this, make sure you provide them with information regarding the discussions, decisions, and intentions that were originally had to shape the character's development. By sharing this context, they can connect with the material on a deeper level and make informed choices that are in sync with the original vision. Without this information, they may feel disconnected from the role and struggle to understand the motivations behind specific actions or emotions. Giving them the tools and insights they need will ultimately lead to a more authentic and compelling performance. If the actor wishes to try a new approach, a quick check-in with the creative team is recommended to ensure approval and avoid any surprises.

It is important you understand the creative team's expectations once a show is opened. Some prefer to be in constant communication with their associates while others will completely step away. If you are not sure of their preference, simply ask and you will have instant clarity.

What Do You Believe Is the Role of an Associate Once a Show Opens and How Do You Maintain It?

- ***Danny Sharron – Associate Director – CABARET AT THE KIT KAT CLUB: Broadway***
  "I like to divide the job into three core parts:

  - *The first is watching and noting the show. This is a way to make sure the quality of the production is sustained over the course of a long run, and also a way to support understudies whenever they perform. Every show requires a different amount of noting . . . for Dear Evan Hansen, I would generally watch/note twice a week; for Cabaret, I would watch/note three times a week.*
  - *The second is casting—which is to say, auditioning replacements for the show. The scale of this can vary based on the show's needs. Casting on Cabaret was minimal as we didn't have to replace too many people over the course of the run. On Dear Evan Hansen, however, we were consistently in casting sessions as we had multiple companies of the show running simultaneously (at one point, four!) and there was always a gap somewhere that needed to be filled.*
  - *The third is rehearsals. Immediately post-opening, rehearsals are mostly focused on getting all of the understudies up to speed as quickly and efficiently as possible. Once that's done, rehearsals become about maintenance and/or very specific problem-solving needs. And then, of course, when you're putting new people into the show you enter a more formal and extended period of rehearsing with those new actors to teach them, and integrate them into, the show.*

  The other major part of the job, which really spans all three of those core parts, has to do with maintaining the wellness of the company. Doing a long run of a show can really take its toll on performers, and I have always felt that a big part of my job is to make sure that the theatre feels like a warm and healthy place, and that the actors feel like they have someone they can talk to about whatever struggles they may be facing. This isn't an official part of the job, per se, but I believe it's important to make sure everyone is taken care of so that they can deliver the kind of performances the show requires (eight times a week!)."

- ***Ashley Rodbro – Associate Director – MOULIN ROUGE!: Broadway***
  "Once a show opens, so much of the job of an associate is to keep the show creatively aligned with what the show was on opening night. That involves many creative and logistical challenges and projects. One major aspect is casting, meaning being present for auditions, running audition work sessions, and building out understudy coverage and coverage charts within different companies and cast sizes. Rehearsals are also a key component of the job. This can mean teaching new company members their roles in a full, multi-week cast

changeover rehearsal process, or it can mean teaching individual people new tracks one at a time as needed. I've had a big role in prioritizing what coverage should be rehearsed when, how, and on what timeline as well, and then executing on those plans, running large and small rehearsals (in studios, onstage, in official put-in rehearsals, etc.). It's also a big part of the job to watch and note the show at night when possible. Ideally, I'll watch a show I'm maintaining several times a week, keeping an eye towards different covers who are onstage, seeing different mixes of performers, and noting the performers to keep the pace, tone, and performances consistent based on the director's initial vision."

Roll Out

When a production achieves critical acclaim, a phase known as a "roll out" can occur. This process involves replicating the original production for new venues or tours. As the original creative teams often move on to other projects, it is usually the associates who will step up to mount each new iteration of the show. This will require you to step into the role of director or choreographer, restaging your creative's work, and you will be expected to ensure the original vision remains completely intact. You will also be responsible to train the local associates or residents who will ensure the show's continued integrity and quality are maintained once you have departed. I navigated this process with *Come From Away,* which went on to have five companies (Toronto, North American tour, Australia, West End, and UK tour) and most recently *Elf,* which started in the West End and went on to have a production on Broadway. I will specifically use my experience with *Elf* to discuss the following points.

Auditions

With choreographer Liam Steel based in London, I assumed responsibility for both the initial Equity chorus calls and the subsequent open calls. My primary job was to narrow down the pool of talent to a core group that would be presented to the creative team during callbacks. I was able to take different dance combinations directly from the show to adjudicate this first few rounds of auditionees, making sure the exact demands of the show were being met. Because the tracks had already been determined, I knew exactly what we were looking for—from specific specialty features and vocal parts to critical understudy assignments. This knowledge allowed casting—Rachel Hoffman and Rashad Naylor—and me to meticulously evaluate the large pool of participants, narrowing it down to a select group of promising candidates.For the final callbacks, we were joined by director Philip Wm. McKinley and choreographer Liam Steel, who would go on to provide their expertise on the final stage of casting. I was able to provide insight from having seen these candidates for several rounds and together we assembled the cast for Broadway.

Preparation

As the costumes, wigs, props, and set went into construction, a dedicated group of American associates joined the team, assuming crucial on-the-ground leadership roles to replicate the original design from London. The flow of information became essential and my responsibility as the Associate Choreographer was to share as much knowledge as I could. Once the Broadway company had been cast, I communicated with the costume department which actor was stepping into which track, including all understudy assignments, confirming all the appropriate costumes were being built. I worked closely with the props department to guarantee that every item being constructed was not only an exact replica but also communicating how they functioned specifically with the choreography. Although these associates could expertly execute the blueprint of what they were being asked to build, they did not necessarily have the knowledge of *how* an item functioned within the show. I also worked closely with our dance captain, Lizz Picini, to prepare her to be as useful as possible during the rehearsal period. This included sharing my Blocking Bible and Stage Write charts as well as an archival video of the West End production. By sharing all available information across every department, it ensured that everyone could contribute effectively from day one and allowed the entire team to be on the same page.

Rehearsals

With choreographer Liam Steel unavailable to attend rehearsals, I was asked to restage his original choreography. I utilized the Blocking Bible, Stage Write charts, and archive footage making necessary modifications, since the Marquis Theatre stage was several feet narrower than the previous West End production at the Dominion Theatre. This smaller footprint required me to adjust the blocking and spacing while preserving the essence of the original work. I was in constant communication with Liam and made sure all adjustments were signed off by him. Crucially, the rehearsal period also served as a comprehensive management handover, training our dance captain Lizz Picini to step into a full managerial role upon my departure following the show's opening night. Lizz's responsibilities included monitoring performances, running understudy rehearsals, taking detailed performance notes, and managing all understudy rehearsals, all while learning the tracks she was responsible for covering as a swing and her principal understudy track.

Post-Opening

Once the production officially opened on Broadway, I remained in close correspondence with the management team on the ground, serving as a resource for any questions. My two years working on the show in the West End allowed me to provide instant clarity on logistical challenges that arose during the run. An example being, should a "cut show" (a performance where there aren't enough cast members to perform all roles originally staged because of illness or holiday) need to occur, I was able to provide immediate, practical guidance having firsthand knowledge on how best to reassign roles, adapt blocking, and guarantee the production remained as close to what was initially conceived as possible. Lizz's exceptional expertise allowed me to step back and hand over the show to her trusting that the production was in good hands. By surrounding yourself with talented and dedicated individuals, it becomes easier to let go and allow them to take the reins, secure in the knowledge that the project will be well protected.

As an associate, ensuring a successful handover is a huge responsibility. Your role includes meticulously equipping the team for success, which begins with the transfer of all documentation—

the detailed Blocking Bible, the Stage Write charts, and all related materials. I make it explicitly clear that although I created these documents, they now belong to the team, and it is their duty to maintain them and make sure they are being looked after. Ways to help protect the intellectual property include sending materials as digital files with password protection. If physical copies are one's preference, clearly label them with the names of who they belong to so that a misplaced document can find its way back. It is a delicate juggling act—granting the new team complete access while simultaneously protecting what has been created, ensuring the integrity of the production is secure long after you have left the building.

Onto the Next

Unlike directors or choreographers who typically conclude their involvement once a show opens, an associate's true demands frequently remain unknown until after opening night. The trajectory of the show, its ongoing needs, and unforeseen requirements dictate the associate's post-opening workload, making it an unpredictable journey.

Associates often find themselves looking for, and potentially securing, their next job before knowing the fate of their current show, to ensure they are employed. While juggling more than one show at a time can be tricky, it is not impossible. I feel that I can comfortably comment on this topic after having been the associate on the Broadway productions of *Come From Away* and the revival of *Company* simultaneously. I was very fortunate because both shows were playing in adjoining theatres, the Gerald Schoenfeld Theatre and the Bernard B. Jacobs Theatre, making travel between very easy. Managing more than one show at a time demands immense organizational skills and a constant dialogue with stage management and the dance captain of both productions, specifically for coordinating a schedule.

The logistics to making this work was very much like figuring out a jigsaw puzzle. A typical week for me would look like the following.

- **Monday:** Dark day for both shows. SLEEP!
- **Tuesday:** Observe the evening performance of *Come From Away*.
- **Wednesday:** Deliver notes to the *Come From Away* company, watch *Come From Away* matinee. Watch the evening performance of *Company.*
- **Thursday:** Afternoon understudy rehearsal for *Company.* Deliver notes before the evening performance to the onstage company, watch the evening performance of *Company.*
- **Friday:** Afternoon understudy rehearsal for *Company.* Deliver notes before the evening performance to the onstage company, watch the evening performance of *Company.*
- **Saturday:** Be available should either show have an understudy go on to observe and take notes.
- **Sunday:** Be available should either show have an understudy go on to observe and take notes.

Inevitably things would come up that would require me to adjust my previously planned schedule requiring me to lean on stage management and the dance captain to hold down the fort. *Come From Away* had been running for some time and was functioning as a well-oiled machine, while *Company* was still in its early stages, with covers needing to go on at the last minute and requiring my immediate attention. Being adaptable and quick to think on my feet allowed me to bounce back and forth between both shows and make sure everyone's needs were being met. Although this busy schedule allowed little opportunity for other work, receiving two separate salaries eliminated the need to take on additional jobs. Ultimately, the success I was able to find managing these two shows simultaneously was because of my meticulous organization and maintaining clear, open lines of communication between both productions.

Although an associate might cultivate an exceptional working relationship with their creative, it's crucial to understand that this bond doesn't guarantee a spot on the next project. Sometimes, a director or choreographer will intentionally *not* bring an associate onto their next show, anticipating that the current show they are working on might demand ongoing maintenance, making them unavailable. Other times, an associate, however talented, simply might not be the right fit for the specific needs required by the next project. These choices, though they may feel disheartening, are made to protect the show the creative is working on and are not indicative of the associate's value or potential.

In a world that often measures success by accolades, credits, and the next big break, it's easy to lose sight of what truly matters—the journey itself. I've learned, through the privilege of working on multiple Broadway shows and countless other projects, that real fulfillment doesn't come from counting how many shows I've done or chasing the next opportunity with relentless ambition. Instead, it comes from showing up fully in each moment, approaching every process as if it were my last. When you operate with that kind of presence, you can't help but give your absolute best. I never allow myself to get comfortable because there is no place for complacency. Every project is a chance to grow, to listen, to learn. Lead with kindness and respect for others and for the work. When it's over, walk away not just with the credit, but with the lessons you have learned.

Balancing Both Sides

Embarking on the journey to become an Associate Director or Choreographer often requires a significant shift in focus. For me, this meant making the conscious decision to step away from performing. My years on stage gave me a deep understanding of the inner workings of theatre—an invaluable foundation that would ultimately inform my transition into a creative role. However, my experience is just one of many. A growing number of associates are successfully navigating the dual roles of performer and creative, proving that choosing one does not necessarily require abandoning the other. This path demands exceptional organizational skills and stamina, as maintaining a show from an associate's perspective while simultaneously fulfilling the rigorous schedule of performing is incredibly intense. Here is some advice from creatives who balance both.

- ***Sarah Parker – Associate Choreographer – CAMELOT: Lincoln Center***
  "I think that working as both an associate and as a performer inform each other in a beautiful way. As someone who still performs, when I become a member of a creative team, I'm able to

offer insight into what the actors/dancers may be experiencing during a certain scene or transition or have a clearer grasp on how to communicate something to the cast. On the flip side, when I am working as a performer, I can bring with me a more well-rounded knowledge of how the creative team is operating. This helps remind me of the big picture and of all the moving parts of the production that actors aren't always privy to. Associate work is much more mentally demanding, while performing is generally more physically demanding, so they provide a nice balance of creativity. If you treat the ability to work on both sides as an advantage and a pathway to deepening your artistry, it will work in your favor. Take what you learn from each experience and use it to expand your understanding of the theatre process as a whole. Let people know that you are open to working in whatever capacity they see you best fit for."

- ***Lizz Picini – Associate Choreographer – The Muny***
  "I absolutely adore the thrill of being both an associate and performer. When I 'wear both hats' I am able to provide valuable insight on multiple fronts. Serving as an essential connection between creative and cast, often results in a more productive, sustainable, efficient process. Understanding how the machine works on 'both sides of the table' makes me stronger as a support to my boss and a performer on stage. While the workload can be challenging, there is nothing more rewarding than smoothly operating as both a respected associate and stunning performer"!

Perspective and Advice

Although I have primarily focused on my experiences, I wanted the perspective and advice from other creatives as well.

What Do You Believe an Associate's Job Is During the Audition, Pre-Production, Rehearsal, and Tech Process?

- ***Rachelle Rak – Associate Choreographer – BOOP!: Broadway***
  "I feel an associate's job is very different for each choreographer's needs. I have watched some associates run the room when the choreographer has to step out. I have watched associates sit back and allow changes to come from the choreographer and take note of those changes, and I have watched choreographers ask an associate to go and fill in a section and help with the creation of the choreography. Again, this is all very personal to the dynamic and trust of the choreographer and their associate.

  During the audition process an Associate Choreographer will sometimes teach the dance combinations for all dance calls. They will work with the choreographer when it's time for the first callbacks or cuts. If the choreographer is not in the room at a dance call, then the associate will make the appropriate suggestions for cuts and sit with the casting agents.

  During pre-pro, which is the time when you, the choreographer, and probably a few dancers go to a studio and work on ideas, an associate can have many jobs. In my experience as an associate on 'Boop!' the musical I would see what Jerry wanted to work on, he always had a list or a plan of things he wanted to touch and ideas he needed to put onto others. I tried to learn it as quickly as possible. It's important to let go of being right when you are asked to do it again. A choreographer can change feet on a second try or changes the idea and the tempo and your job is to catch it. They are not usually interested in what foot they started on. It was not easy at first because I am wired to remember things as much as I can exactly how they were done, but when you are creating it's important to remember to let that go. I think it's best to follow along, video a lot of the rehearsal and when you leave the room you can go home and review what was created that day. The associate should know the work from every day of pre- pro and into rehearsal. Things change all the time, my best advice is to not get set on one version, there are usually many more versions coming your way. Also, in pre-pro you may be asked to share some ideas or some combinations of your own, depending on the choreographer you are working with and the show and if you have a particular skill they need. Wait for it. Do your work at home, you may get to show it to the choreographer and teach it to the dancers. So, always be ready and if the opportunity presents itself, take it. You have nothing to lose.

In rehearsal an associate is constantly documenting ideas, choreography and changes. This is also the first time you have your actual cast and there is a lot to take in. I would recommend memorizing everyone's name and ask for a full company photo sheet prior to the first day of rehearsal. It helped me to know who I was working with, and it made it easier to teach the steps and begin staging. It can slow you down if you don't know everyone's name. It also sets the tone for the room. The rehearsal process is a sacred space. It is important to be a positive representative of the dance department and have the ability to give notes and create a safe environment. When you are the one running the rehearsal, you represent the choreographer. I think it's good to know what that means to you.

The tech process can be grueling on everyone. Your job as an associate is to sit with the director and choreographer, or just the choreographer depending on the team, and get up and down and give notes on blocking. When you tech a show it is to cue and that means everyone has to be on the exact mark because we are setting lights, as well as sound, and set pieces are moving. This is an important time to rely on your stage managers and the stage crew to learn about what is actually allowed to happen on stage. Everything changes during tech. This is the time you sort of give over to the show and all of the elements and you don't always get the time to clean up dances or dance segments even though you want to. I have heard people say many times during tech that it's when you lose the show for a bit and then you get it back. Tech is a great time to get your documenting updated and make minor changes to your notes of your Stage Write, or whatever method you use."

- ***Cedric Dodd – Associate Choreographer – THE GREAT GATSBY: Broadway***
  "As an associate, your job is to be an extension of the choreographer. Every choreographer works and creates differently so your job is to understand their process and see how you can infuse your work ethic with theirs.

  The job of an associate is multifaceted.

  A standard part of the job might be to clean a number from the show and help adjust spacing on stage. You may be tasked with going backstage to help with orchestrating a quick change. There will be times that your job is to lead the room while the choreographer steps into a meeting and other times you are the person to help unlock an idea for the choreographer by providing a fresh set of eyes on the material.

It's important to develop trust and respect not only with the choreographer but every member of the production. The cast, crew, or other creative team members may come to you to help them solve a problem knowing that you will provide an answer that would be approved by the choreographer, so they can continue to move forward. In those moments, your job is to help find a solution all while keeping the integrity of the choreographer in mind. The decision you make reflects strongly upon both of you since you are an extension of them.

On a personal level, I think one of the most important parts of your job is to be a person for the choreographer to lean on when they need to. You are the person they chose to sit next to for hours while working in a cold dark theatre. You are going to be in auditions, rehearsals, production meetings, and tech together. Most times, the job starts well before the first day of rehearsal and may continue on long after opening night. Your job is to continue to uphold the vision that was developed in a living room and made its way all the way to the stage."

- **DB Bonds – Associate Director – KINKY BOOTS: Broadway**
  "I believe the most important thing that I do as an associate is to be a trustworthy sounding board. I have been Jerry Mitchell's Associate Director for many years. Jerry trusts my opinions and knows that I will tell him the truth.

  I also think it's important to know when to not speak. There may be times where you believe something might not work, but you don't want to interrupt the creation of something by inserting your opinions at the wrong time. I want to do everything possible to support the director's process. I am always ready with an opinion when asked. I believe that it's important to know the right time to give those opinions."

What Advice Would You Give to an Aspiring Associate?

- ***Rachelle Rak – Associate Choreographer – BOOP!: Broadway***
  "The best advice I can offer an aspiring associate is to swing a show or dance captain a show to learn how all of the elements work. If you have the skillset to remember and teach and you love the idea of possibly stepping out of performing and into being an associate those skills will help you. It's not the only path of course, but just an idea. If you think you are interested in working with someone who perhaps choreographed a show you were in and you like them and love the way they work, then simply inquire and maybe ask about it. I will tell you this little personal story. Someone asked me if Jerry just asked me to be an associate on 'Boop.' I laughed and said, I pitched myself for seven years and every year I would meet for lunch or a visit and he would ask me what I was working on or what ideas I had and I would tell him and he would say what else and I would continue to pitch other ideas. I didn't know I wanted to be an associate until I did and when I did, I had to keep trying. It took years of making reels and teaching classes and working on new ideas for myself. Finally, a show came into my life and the seven-year pitch was over. 'Boop'! the

musical was my first associate title on Broadway and even though it didn't last long, I know that I worked and waited and did the work. I was fortunate to see a lot of choreography that I created with Jerry on that stage and the three years I spent on Boop! was an absolute gift. Oh, I forgot, as an associate sometimes you get to work with a new and up and coming star named Jasmine Amy Rogers and my time with her was worth the entire process. Now, do the work and go get 'em. I'm cheering you on."

- ***Cedric Dodd – Associate Choreographer – THE GREAT GATSBY: Broadway***

  "Advice I believe is important to remember is to make sure you enjoy the process and also find ways to be a human throughout.

  Remember that your process might be different from others around you. Stay open to learning new ways to execute certain tasks and incorporate what you find works best for you.

  You are a human. You may have all the answers to the questions that are asked of you or you may have to say, let me get back to you. Remember, either reply is okay.

  After a long day of rehearsals, it is important to press pause on your work responsibilities for a bit to enjoy life. It is necessary to take a break to refocus and clear your mind. Taking a moment to sit in the stillness of this time, will help you be a better associate for the production and most importantly for yourself."

- ***DB Bonds – Associate Director – KINKY BOOTS: Broadway***

  "If you are wanting to be an associate, I think you should write to directors or choreographers that you admire. I was an actor for many years and had worked with Jerry Mitchell several times.

  I also think that it's important to be a people person. Part of my job is to get Jerry's message to actors. It's important that they trust me as well. Sometimes, being an associate can be about how to deal with different personalities. You have to change the way you communicate with different people based on their ability to hear certain things. Being intuitive is vital."

PART THREE
ON THE JOB (PLAYS)

Perspective and Advice

Having been an associate who has exclusively worked on musicals, I wanted to get the insight from several trusted colleagues who work on plays.

How Do You Think Working as an Associate Director on a Play Might Be Different from Working on a Musical?

- ***Kasey RT Graham: Associate Director – ART: Broadway***
  "These are definitely broad strokes, as these days so many musicals feel like plays and a number of plays move and look like musicals. The main difference is the number of creatives involved. Generally speaking, there are more cooks in the kitchen (in the best possible sense) in a musical. As an Associate Director, you're not only assisting the director but acting as a liaison, messenger, interpreter, and sometimes therapist between the director and the other departments. There are simply more departments on musicals, which means your focus is split in more directions.

  Another broad-stroke answer is that musicals will often run longer than plays, so an associate's job in the long run becomes much more about maintenance and care-taking of a show over the months or years it runs. Often a director will only get back to see a show every few months, if that, so it's the job of the associates, along with the stage management team, to ensure a production remains as true to the original incarnation as possible."
- ***Tavia Rivée Jefferson – Associate Director – STRANGER THINGS: THE FIRST SHADOW: Broadway***
  "Working on a play is different because there's usually less collaboration once the creative team steps away. On a play, the Associate Director often becomes the main artistic voice in the room, maintaining the tone and integrity of the piece on their own.

  In a musical, you're in conversation with the choreography and music teams. Everyone's work overlaps, so you're collaborating to make sure the story, movement, and music are all telling the same story.

  Both setups have their benefits. A play can feel like there are less cooks, but I enjoy the teamwork that comes with musicals—it makes the job feel less solitary."

- ***Conner Wilson – Associate Director – WAITING FOR GODOT: Broadway***
  "I find working on a play as an associate a different sort of challenge than a musical. With a musical; many of the climatic show stopping moments are fixed in space and time. Of course there is the freedom of individual expression; however, an actor can either hit the final note of 'Defying Gravity' or they can't. In a play—the moments of peak emotional tension are not limited by what a score has dictated. When Romeo says 'Thus with a kiss I die,' the room for dramatic interpretation is simply as vast as human language will allow. The challenge after the show opens then becomes: 1) How do we preserve the emotional integrity of this climactic moment (without the guardrails of a score)? 2) How do the understudies replicate this—without the choice feeling artificial or second-hand. Plays have quite a bit of emotional and physical freedom; with that freedom comes its own sort of artistic challenges."

What Are the Responsibilities of an Associate Director on a Play from Auditions up Till Opening Night?

- ***Kasey RT Graham: Associate Director – ART: Broadway***
  "These responsibilities can vary widely depending on the director for whom you're the associate. Some directors lean heavily on their associates during every stage of the process, while others utilize them more intensely during the rehearsal and tech process. My experiences have run the gamut, but here are some of the duties an associate can be called upon to execute:

  During the pre-production stages, an associate might sit in on design meetings and keep organized notes on the scenic, costume, lighting, and properties designs. At auditions duties can range from being a sounding board for the director to running preliminary calls with the casting agents, narrowing down the field of auditioners for the director to see later in the process.

  In the lead-up to the first rehearsal I've been called upon to compile and organize research, create glossaries, communicate with the stage management team and actors, and anything else that might be helpful for the director. Anticipating needs (and then meeting them) is a good rule of thumb for any associate.

  Once rehearsals begin it becomes about notating anything and everything you can: blocking, dramatic intentions, action, bits of backstory created. I always approach this part of the process with the knowledge that one of an associate's main duties is to rehearse understudies and future replacements. Every bit of information you can gather and notate here will pay off exponentially down the line.

  As you move into the tech and preview process, the focus irises out to include more of the other departments. While you are taking notes for the director, you are also an extra set of eyes and ears, helping to bring issues to the director's attention. Taking and distributing notes during tech is a crucial part of the job so work on your handwriting in the dark. :)

  After a show opens, the responsibilities become about maintenance and morale. If you're lucky enough to work on a long-running show it seems like both can become full-time jobs.

Whether it's rehearsing understudies/replacements or keeping a company's focus on stage sharp, maintaining and honoring the director's vision is priority number one."

- ***Tavia Rivée Jefferson – Associate Director – STRANGER THINGS: THE FIRST SHADOW: Broadway***

  "As an Associate Director, my biggest responsibility from auditions through opening is to learn as much as I can about the director's vision so I can carry it forward.

  During auditions, I listen for how they describe the characters and what draws them to certain performers. In rehearsal, I'm focused on how they shape scenes, what details matter to them, and how they communicate with the company. I'm also notating blocking and tracking adjustments, but the real work is absorbing the 'why' behind their choices.

  This knowledge becomes essential once I start running understudy rehearsals—often during tech—and later when I help audition replacements. The more I take in early on, the better I can support the show and keep it aligned with what the director originally set."

- ***Conner Wilson – Associate Director – WAITING FOR GODOT: Broadway***

  "Before the play opens, a great deal of the associate's job is absorption. Much like the director and actor are in a dialogue about character; the director and associate are in a dialogue about what the play itself wants to be. The associate's job is to document the way in which the story unfolds through all its various iterations until the clear path forward emerges. This intense and deep knowledge of the material allows the director to pass the reins over at opening night; knowing the full journey of the play lives in the associate's mind. Alongside this there is also, of course, the usual responsibilities of: note-taking, blocking books, creative meetings, understudy rehearsals—or whatever the director may call on the associate to help out with."

What Advice Would You Give to an Aspiring Associate Director?

- ***Kasey RT Graham: Associate Director – ART: Broadway***

  "My advice for an aspiring associate is suss out as quickly as possible the kind of associate that director needs and wants. If you know someone who's worked with them before, take them out for a quick coffee, and pick their brain. Have a conversation with the director early on and ask how they like to work. Be as useful as you can be. And make friends with the stage management team. You'll work more closely with them than almost anyone else. Make yourself someone the artist people want to work with again and again."

PART FOUR
INHERITING A SHOW AS AN ASSOCIATE

Joining a transfer of a show as an associate presents a unique challenge. When I joined the Broadway production of *Company* as the US Associate Choreographer working alongside choreographer Liam Steel and original West End Associate Choreographer Simone Sault, I faced the following dilemma: *How do you foster a genuine sense of ownership over a show that has already been fully conceived and executed long before your involvement?*

Knowing this would be a very new experience for me, my approach was to be as prepared as possible. My work began the instant I was hired: I requested an archive and all available documentation from the original West End production. These materials became my day-and-night study. Crucially, I did not stop at just watching and studying what was given to me; I built my own comprehensive Blocking Bible and started making my own Stage Write charts. This process of viewing the existing materials that had been sent to me and then documenting it for myself forced me to get the show both in my brain and body.

Although this initial deep dive wouldn't teach me all the specific intricacies of the show, it certainly helped me familiarize myself as much as I could. This preparation allowed me to walk into rehearsals prepared to start absorbing and understanding everything Liam was saying while simultaneously finding my footing. Liam's confidence in me was quickly evident when he began delegating me different responsibilities including sending me to lead cleaning rehearsals while his focus was required elsewhere. This hands-on experience proved to be incredibly helpful in forcing me to see how well I knew the material and to what level of detail I could explain it, while also building a relationship with the company, since I would ultimately be managing the show once Liam returned to London. When questions arose that I couldn't immediately answer, I maintained absolute transparency, promising to confer with Liam as soon as possible to secure the accurate answer.

Although I occasionally felt isolated given my lack of history with the show and the creative team, I actively reminded myself that our current process was creating new memories, and that the team and I were discovering unique, specific moments relevant only to this production. A sense of confidence proved instrumental to navigating this challenging, fast-paced process. Forcing myself to trust my instincts allowed me a sense of comfort and ownership over the material. After a period of time I felt that I had absorbed all I needed to know to comfortably step into a full leadership position once Liam and Simone both left the production.

When I joined *Titanique* in the West End as Associate Director and Choreographer, I was once again stepping into a production with an established history and multiple prior iterations. Drawing on my experience with *Company*, I approached the role with a clearer understanding of how to navigate the demands of such a process. Having seen the show Off-Broadway, I already had valuable context for what I was stepping into. Balancing both directorial and choreographic responsibilities required constant focus. I had to keep my attention on both director Tye Blue and choreographer Ellenore Scott, ensuring I absorbed as much information as possible. By this stage, they had mounted the show numerous times and operated with a rhythm that was highly organized and fast-paced. They transitioned seamlessly between directing and choreography, maintaining a steady flow throughout the rehearsal room. At the end of each day, I often returned home mentally exhausted, processing an overwhelming amount of information.

As with *Company*, it took some time to fully feel part of the team. However, having an existing relationship with both Tye and Ellenore helped accelerate that process. By consistently asking questions and engaging in the work, I was able to build my confidence and their trust. By the time the show opened, I felt prepared to step into a leading creative role and help steer the production forward.

How Is Being an Associate on a Show That Has Already Been Created Different and What Advice Would You Give to Someone Stepping into This Role?

- ***Ashley Andrews – Associate Choreographer – SUNSET BOULEVARD: Broadway***
  "The biggest difference being an associate on a show that has already been created is that for the most part the creativity has been done. For many shows it takes years for the idea of the show to become a reality. As a result, the creative team attached to the project was formed quite some time ago working closely together to create the story they want to tell. Over this time, they form a creative bond. Each one of them has had a part in how the show came to life and has ownership over the work. It can be difficult to join a team at a later stage in the process. When you join a project from the ground up you are there with them in the trenches developing the world you want to create, and as such, you have ownership in its creation. Therefore, I would say with an original show there is ownership while inheriting an already realized show is more about management.

  ADVICE: *Ask questions! With every new project or creative relationship comes the opportunity to learn and grow, and like any relationship, the only way for it to thrive is to have clear communication, understanding, and respect. I find it best to help myself by understanding as much as I can about the choreographer I am working for. What is their background? Where did they train? What influences them? Who have they worked for in the past? Find out if they have any particular things that they like or don't like. Asking questions about their process will help you understand how best you can facilitate their vision.*

  For me an important quality to understand is their boundaries as well as your own. All choreographers are different and all associates are different. Not every choreographer is meant for every associate and vice versa. For example, I worked with one choreographer who always wanted me by their side at every moment. Whereas another choreographer felt suffocated if their associate was all over them the whole time. It is a balance and sometimes without clear communication it can feel emotionally exhausting to feel unsettled in the creative space. If there is doubt it is because there is uncertainty. Uncertainty shows us there is a gap in our knowledge. How do we fill that gap? The answer is with knowledge. How do we gain knowledge? Ask questions!! It's simple really. Keep the dialogue open. With this will come understanding and then the flow between creatives can thrive."

PART FIVE
BROADWAY vs. REGIONAL THEATRE

Although my narrative so far has been focused specifically on Broadway shows, stepping into the role of an associate at a regional theatre is a very similar experience. The core duties of supporting the creative team and facilitating the production process are largely the same. There are, however, some differences.

The casting process benefits from a more streamlined approach, given that most regional venues stage already known titles. This means going into the audition process there is a clearer understanding of what is needed for each role. On Broadway, the standard practice is to have two understudies per role, however most regional theatres only employ one understudy, easing some of the demands typically placed on the ensemble. Regional theatres often begin their casting process with an initial "open call," where the candidates auditioning are being considered for the entire upcoming season. Because these calls are not limited to a single production, multiple creative teams are typically present, and the number of hopefuls can be overwhelming, often exceeding 500 individuals.

For an associate, stepping into this room demands paramount preparation and organization. Clear notes detailing track breakdowns, character requirements, and vocal ranges allows the team to observe potential candidates knowing exactly what is needed to fill each role. As you begin to audition the potential hopefuls, they will start to fall into certain categories of where they might potentially fit in the show (a lead dance track, a character role that plays several different parts, a principal understudy). Although the casting director will be incredibly helpful in organizing the potential hopefuls during the casting sessions, your intricate detailed notes will help as the pool begins to narrow down.

Because most of these theatres cast quite far in advance, there is a possibility you will need to replace an actor before the show goes into production because of them booking another gig, so make sure you hold onto your notes, that they are detailed, and that you can offer a possible replacement quickly.

For casting principal roles, there is a scenario where an actor is considered "offer only," meaning they will receive a direct offer without an audition. This usually occurs when an actor has previously performed the specific role on Broadway, on tour, or at another regional theatre, or when an actor with substantial credits is specifically being approached by the theatre. When making an offer based solely on reputation and resume, without the benefit of an in-person audition, the creative team must unanimously feel confident in the actor's skill set to ensure they are making the right casting decision.

Although the rehearsal process itself functions like its Broadway counterpart, the timeline tends to be much more compressed. Some regional theatres will bring a show from first rehearsal to opening night in less than two weeks, including staging, technical rehearsals, and previews. This fast-paced schedule emphasizes the importance of the pre-production period, prompting more and more theatres to budget for and implement dedicated time before rehearsals even begin. Shows are built much differently now, usually requiring the full company's presence in most rehearsals, making separating the room less feasible than in the past. Furthermore, the nature of a regional production—often performed at one theatre without a planned roll out—also influences the scope of documentation needed. Although thorough records remain essential, they typically don't demand the exhaustive detail of a Broadway Blocking Bible. However, this isn't universally true. Instances where several regional theatres collaborate on a single show, functioning almost as a mini-tour, where a physical production transfers but a new cast is hired, require more detailed and comprehensive documentation to ensure a seamless remounting and consistent artistic vision across venues.

Regional theatres tend to require you to be more resourceful and innovative since they are operating on drastically smaller budgets compared to Broadway shows. For instance, since most regional theatres don't have automation, this means that scenic transitions will rely on cast and crew to push pieces on and off stage instead of using mechanical tracks. Every transition must be meticulously staged and choreographed and must be achievable and repeatable within the show's tight tech timeline. This requires an intensive pre-planning phase, identifying every piece of moving scenery in a singular transition and how it operates. Being able to mock this up as close as possible during studio rehearsals will help save time during tech.

As an associate, my role during the rehearsal process becomes substantially more encompassing. Before rehearsals even begin, I collaborate closely with the director or choreographer to build detailed rehearsal lists, including what necessary scenic elements, props, and costumes, or their stand-ins, are needed in the rehearsal room. This early integration not only benefits the actors but also allows the creative team to comment on what is being proposed and allows time for adjustments long before tech begins. Once rehearsal starts, beyond fulfilling what is normally asked of you during this period, you are also dealing with designers in a much more detailed way that would typically be reserved for the tech process on a Broadway show. This means you are basically taking two highly detailed periods of a show's creative process and putting them into one. Email will become your best friend. You'll be sending and responding to emails at a furious pace to ensure every individual's creative process remains uninterrupted and efficient. This intense front-loading of effort during rehearsals is key to a smoother, less stressful technical period for everyone involved.

An associate's daily check-in with each department is crucial. Personally relaying detailed rehearsal notes—even if they are already included in stage management's daily report—helps address questions and ensures departments can make immediate adjustments. Throughout the rehearsal process, an associate's documentation must be meticulously updated and instantly accessible to all departments via platforms such as Dropbox or Google Docs, guaranteeing everyone is working off the same paperwork. The fast pace of a regional theatre rehearsal process often means the director and choreographer are being pulled in many different directions, leaving the associate with the responsibility of making sure every bit of information is accurately passed on to its intended recipient. I have found that creating checklists throughout the day is a helpful tool. It allows me to organize the information clearly, and every time I have completed a note, being able to check it off ensures it has been passed on and nothing has slipped through the cracks.

With technical rehearsals typically being only a few days, minimizing surprises is essential for a smooth transition from the rehearsal room to the stage. One significant advantage of regional theatres is the close proximity of their design offices and workshops, allowing creatives to witness progress in real time. This makes it easier to catch potential issues early on: a prop built too heavy for an actor to lift, a set door hinged in the wrong direction, or a skirt that needs a slit for the choreography to be executed correctly. Additionally, having designers on-site allows them to observe rehearsals. They themselves can flag any discrepancies from their original vision and make necessary revisions before tech.

One of the most important aspects of creating a smooth tech process involves protecting actors from the information overload that often accompanies being on stage for the first time. The integration of sets, lights, costumes, wigs, and sound can be incredibly overwhelming, which makes introducing as many practical elements as possible directly into the rehearsal room incredibly important. This concept significantly cuts down on the actors' learning curve, minimizing introducing new things once the production begins tech.

Once a regional production has opened, it is common for the associate to depart almost immediately, leaving the day-to-day maintenance and understudy rehearsals to the stage management team and dance captain. A regional show typically runs for only a few weeks, which means understudy rehearsal is scarce. Recognizing the breakneck speed at which blocking, choreography, and staging information is conveyed during rehearsals, I always share my Blocking Bible and Stage Write charts with the understudies, whether I am the associate or the lead creative. Providing these resources helps them navigate their process with greater specificity and confidence. By giving them every resource possible, if and when they are called upon to step into a role, they are prepared for success.

PART SIX
EXPERIENCES AROUND THE WORLD

After having spent the past few years living in London, I've gained a unique vantage point of some differences between theatre in the UK and the United States.

Auditions

The audition landscape in the UK, at least in my experience, presents a distinct contrast to what one might encounter in the United States, particularly concerning open calls and chorus calls. In the UK, the process is by appointment only, highlighting the critical role of agents in an actor's success. The typical order of events involves a show's breakdown being circulating, after which agents submit their clients to the casting directors. These casting directors then meticulously curate a group they believe aligns with the creative team's guidelines, and this is where the audition process begins for the creative team. This system comes with advantages. By immediately working with a smaller group, the team can dedicate more time and focused attention to each auditionee from the outset, allowing for a deeper exploration of everyone's capabilities. However, a significant drawback is the potential exclusion of talent—individuals who might be perfect for a role but lack agency representation or direct connections with casting directors may not get the chance to be seen.

Audition rooms in the UK rarely see the sheer numbers typical of a Broadway casting session. When building a cast for a Broadway production, we often have extensive backup lists; in the UK, however, the backup list is never as deep, simply because you will see a smaller group of talent.

Rehearsals

While the rehearsal and tech process remain remarkably similar on both sides of the Atlantic, the underlying structure of the workday is differentiated most clearly by breaks and length of call. Under US Equity rules, the schedule is defined by frequent breaks, with artists usually taking a five-minute break after fifty-five minutes of work, or a slightly longer ten-minute break after an hour and twenty minutes. The UK's West End system is structured around a fifteen-minute break every three hours known as "tea breaks." These breaks typically occur once mid-morning and once in the post-lunch session. Nothing feels more quintessentially British than a break with a group of artists convening over a cup of tea and biscuits.

Cast Changes

The West End theatre operates under a different employment model than Broadway, where the company is typically contracted for a full year with no option to leave mid-run. This means that everyone, from leads to ensemble members, will start and end their contracts on the same date, resulting in a consistent cast for the duration of the year. Most Broadway contracts allow actors to give notice and depart after a notice period of four to eight weeks. The West End's approach eliminates the possibility of rehearsing in new actors during the run, as the current cast is committed for the full year. As the contract period comes to a close, the actors will make it known if they would like to stay on for another year and the producers will approach those who they would like to have stay. Once it is known who is staying and who is leaving, new casting begins for the roles that need to be replaced. The new company members undergo a designated rehearsal process before being integrated with the returning cast members. The current company will complete their contracts on their designated end date and the next performance will feature the new company (some returning cast members and some new ones).

Warm-up

All shows in the UK do a compulsory warm-up led by the dance captain, music director, or resident. Actors are called ninety minutes before show time and will be led through a physical and vocal warm-up followed by parish notes. There is then a window for anyone on the management team to address any notes regarding the show. This could include a quick clean up on a specific number or could be putting in an understudy who will be making their debut that night into key moments. I personally love this system because it allows the company to come together as one before the performance. This is a fantastic way to gauge the energy in the building and for the company to connect with each other before going on stage. On Broadway, there are some theatres where the dressing rooms are so spread out that you will not see your fellow company members until you are on stage in a scene with them. Another perk to this system is it cuts down on the need to call clean-up rehearsals outside of show hours. Although it does make for a longer time in the theatre for the actors, I believe it offers essential perks that make it worth it. Additionally, similar to the Broadway system, actors in the West End are not allowed to get notes after half-hour, which makes this additional time before the show incredibly useful in distributing notes.

Run of Shows

Show longevity between Broadway and London's West End is a direct reflection of the differing financial ecosystems in which they operate. Broadway is fundamentally a more high-stakes commercial market, demanding aggressive revenue from the beginning. The capital investment required to mount a major production in New York—encompassing union labor costs, theatre rent, and marketing campaigns—is significantly higher than its West End counterpart. This high financial "nut" forces Broadway shows to hit a much higher weekly revenue merely to stay operational, let alone begin the process of recouping their initial investment. If a production fails to meet these box office demands almost immediately, the financial risk becomes unmanageable, leading to the quick issuance of a "closing notice." Although the West End remains highly commercial, the generally lower operational overhead and reduced pressure for rapid recoupment allows struggling shows more flexibility in which they can weather slow periods and build an audience over time, a luxury rarely afforded on the high-cost, hyper-leveraged stages of Broadway.

Stage Management

One of the most significant learning curves I encountered upon joining the West End theatre community was an understanding of how the stage management team operates. Coming from the States, I was accustomed to a particular set of titles and a defined hierarchy within the stage management department, most notably the clear distinction between the stage manager and assistant stage managers. In the West End, while the core responsibilities of ensuring the smooth running of a production remain, the specific titles and duties varied.

The **Deputy Stage Manager** is a key figure in theatre production who runs rehearsals and calls the cues for all technical elements during performances. During the rehearsal period, the deputy stage manager is the director's right hand, seated alongside them to meticulously document every detail of the developing show. They capture all actor blocking, constructing the comprehensive "prompt copy," the master script that will become the definitive blueprint for the production, integrating blocking, technical cues, and all other essential information. The deputy stage manager is also responsible for creating logistical paperwork, from detailed entrance and exit plots, props setting lists, to critical quick changes. They are the primary communicative force working very closely with the stage manager to draft daily rehearsal notes for all departments and outlining the essential rehearsal call for each day.

Once the production moves into the theatre, the deputy stage manager becomes the crucial voice that "calls the show," dictating *what* happens and *when*. This involves precisely coordinating every technical cue—lighting changes, sound effects, scene shifts, and performer entrances—to seamlessly bring the creative image to life as viewed from the audience. They maintain a primary focus on the overall flow of the show working with the stage manager for direct oversight of onstage elements and the assistant stage managers who handle the immediate, hands-on logistics. In essence, the DSM operates the machine.

The **Stage Manager** heads the stage management department and orchestrates the entire show directly from the stage. During a performance, their eye is vital, spotting every precise scenery move, ensuring the flawless and safe execution of cues, and serving as the immediate responder and coordinator when the unexpected occurs. They are, ultimately, the person responsible for the technical integrity and smooth running of the show once it opens. By connecting with the large number of technical teams and departments, the stage manager ensures the creative ideal is realized and sustained. Unlike a Stage Manager in the US, this role in the UK does not involve giving acting notes to performers; that responsibility lies with the Resident Director.

The **Assistant Stage Manager** supports the stage management team, assisting with administrative and practical tasks before and during performances, functioning in a role very similar to that in the States. Their work starts well before the audience arrives with the setting and dressing of all props, ensuring every item is precisely positioned and ready for use. During the performance, the assistant stage manager is responsible for orchestrating the swift and safe execution of scene changes within their area, managing the movement of crew members, and facilitating any necessary stage business.

College Showcases

The culmination of most musical theatre training programs in the States is a college showcase—a revue often performed at their school and then in New York City, designed to give each graduate a moment in the spotlight showcasing their talent through singing, dance, and acting for agents and casting directors to see them. In the UK, the experience is dramatically different. For starters, most colleges are a three-year program and instead of a traditional showcase, they mount full-scale plays and/or musicals. These colleges spare no expense, dedicating substantial budgets for high-quality sets, lighting, costumes, and—most importantly—hiring leading industry creatives to direct and choreograph, often budgeting for the creatives to bring on an associate. Having been fortunate enough to direct and choreograph several of these final year musicals, I find the experience incredibly fulfilling. It offers these artists a real-life experience of what it means to put on a show. The rehearsal process, which I treat as I would any professional show, is a fantastic way to witness the student's growth all the way through to opening night. This training allows graduates to enter the professional world equipped not just with their individual talent, but with a comprehensive grasp of what it takes to put on a show and having already established relationships with key industry figures. Many of these college productions are helmed by West End Associate Directors and Choreographers, giving them the opportunity to showcase their lead creative work on a professional level.

Caitlin Brightey, Harry Parkinson, Kara Roberts, and Paige-Marie Donoghue in *Footloose* at Bird College.
Credit: Courtesy of Bird College, photo by Becky Lee

The Company of *Footloose* at Bird College.
Credit: Courtesy of Bird College, photo by Becky Lee

PART SEVEN
CONTRACTS

It might surprise you to learn that the Stage Directors and Choreographers Society (SDC) only recently, in 2023, established a landmark associate contract for Broadway productions, first-class tours, and other Broadway League development activities. This groundbreaking SDC and Broadway League Agreement extends crucial union protections to associates. For the first time, these individuals received invaluable benefits, including health and pension contributions, marking a significant step towards equitable treatment and professional stability in a demanding industry. Although this represents a monumental stride, the landscape for associates in regional theatre remains more varied, with some theatres creating their own specific contracts that are not yet fully recognized or standardized by SDC. Nevertheless, SDC stands as an essential resource, offering invaluable advocacy and protection for its members and aspiring associates in direction and choreography. You would be wise to explore the organization's offerings and membership, as it continues to shape a more secure and professional future for the industry's creative talent.

https://sdcweb.org/faq/does-sdc-cover-associate-and-assistant-work-on-a-contract/

Does SDC cover Associate and Assistant work on a contract?
SDC currently covers Associate work in the following jurisdictions:

- **Broadway & First-Class Tours**
  - **If you are an Associate Member or Full Member working as an Associate or Resident on a Broadway production or first-class tour, the elective SDC Associate Contract is available for you to request. If secured, Associate Members are required to upgrade to Full Membership prior to the effective date of their contract.**

- **Non-Equity Tours**
  - **If you are a Full Member working as an Associate on a Non-Equity Tour, the producer is required to file an SDC contract for your work.**
  - **If you are working as a Restager on a Non-Equity Tour, regardless of your Membership status, the producer is required to cover you on an SDC contract. This contract requires that you join SDC or upgrade to Full Membership prior to the first rehearsal date.**

- Regional Musical Theatre
  - **If you are a Full Member working as an Associate or Assistant at a theatre covered by the Regional Musical Theatre Agreement, the theatre is required to file an SDC contract for your work.**

When entering into an associate contract, several key elements should be clearly defined to ensure you are protected and being taken care of. This will include **Engagement and services**, which meticulously details the specific duties and responsibilities of each party. This section will outline the scope of work, the obligations expected of the associate, and those expected of the producers. Secondly, the **Term** of the contract is crucial, typically encompassing dates from the initial rehearsal period, through the first performance, and concluding with opening night. Any required attendance at auditions or pre-production meetings should also be explicitly stated. **Compensation** is another required point, usually stipulating a weekly fee during rehearsals and a day rate once the production opens. Some contracts might structure payment as a "fee" distributed in instalments, such as one-third upon signing, one-third at the commencement of rehearsals, and the final third on opening night. Furthermore, **Billing** provisions are essential, specifying the associate's official title, the placement of this credit (e.g., title page, staff page), and any accompanying biographical information. Finally, the contract should include details for **Opening night**, typically including the number of complimentary tickets provided to the associate and party passes should one be occurring.

COMPENSATION: Let's be clear: the path of an associate is not designed to make you rich. When I was first starting out, I wasn't in a position to command high fees, as I was still building my resume and establishing my reputation in the industry, which often required me to hustle. I frequently supplemented my income by teaching classes, judging dance competitions, and setting pieces at dance studios around the country—anything that provided financial support while keeping my schedule flexible for creative work. It isn't always glamorous and there are times you will be completely exhausted trying to make ends meet. But if this is indeed what you want to do, it will all be worth it. It wasn't until further into my career when established creatives demanded that I be included on their team that my agent and I found ourselves in a position to push back for a more substantial fee. The art of negotiating is a tricky one: making sure you are never being taken advantage of but also honoring the time it takes to build your reputation and clout in the industry.

EXPENSES AND REIMBURSEMENTS: When negotiating a contract that requires out-of-town travel, it is essential to ensure all associated expenses are clearly outlined and included. This typically encompasses transportation, accommodation, and per diem for daily living costs. The expected duration of your travel often influences the class of service offered for flights. For extended or international journeys, advocating for a comfort or business-class seat is highly recommended. This allows for better rest and minimizes the physical toll of long-haul flights, enabling you to be more productive and focused upon arrival. Furthermore, attaching yourself with a preferred airline and hotel and requesting its use for company travel can be useful. Accumulating loyalty points can lead to personal travel benefits down the line.

It is essential to remember that you shouldn't have to bear the financial burden of any expenses related to your role. Whether it is a specialized app such as Stage Write, travel costs, script copies, or any other resource necessary for doing your job effectively, always feel empowered to seek reimbursement. Early in my career, while working on *Newsies*, I purchased Stage Write to help document the show. Recognizing that this tool was directly benefiting the production, I submitted my receipt—and was reimbursed. If a company expects you to maintain accurate records or use specific tools to fulfill your responsibilities, it is only fair that they cover the cost. Too often, associates hesitate to submit expenses, fearing they'll come across as being difficult. But advocating for yourself isn't being a nuisance—it's asserting your professional worth.

ADDITIONAL HOURS: When negotiating contracts, it is incredibly wise to establish a clear day rate, offering you protection should work extend beyond the specified dates listed on your initial agreement. This pre-agreed rate guarantees fair compensation for your time. A straightforward and equitable method to derive this amount is to take your standard weekly salary and divide it by six, providing a daily figure that reflects the value of your time and expertise. I have often included a half-day fee in my contracts for workdays under eight hours, typically calculated as half of my daily rate. Establishing this from the outset provides an added layer of protection.

Once a production officially opens and the creative team has departed, associates often step into more leadership roles that go well beyond their original job descriptions. No longer simply supporting the creative you are working with, you are now responsible for maintaining the integrity of the production, solving emergent issues, and guiding the cast and crew independently. Given this substantial increase in responsibility, it is both reasonable and fair to negotiate a higher day rate at this stage. Compensation should reflect not just the duties outlined in a contract, but the actual scope of leadership and oversight required. Advocating for increased pay acknowledges the added pressure and professional skill involved in successfully sustaining a production on your own.

BILLING: For an associate, securing title page billing is very important. Although a bio is usually included in the program, having an associate's name appear on the title page validates their contribution by placing them on the same page as key production personnel. Every associate should be prepared to advocate for this. Associates are frequently the first group placed on the short list of people deemed expendable from the title page, minimizing the importance of their work. It is crucial to understand that allowing this omission minimizes the scope of your work. Always stand your ground here; your efforts, expertise, and dedication merit the official acknowledgment of title page inclusion, ensuring you receive the credit due as an integral member of the creative team.

AGENT: The sooner an associate can sign with an agent, the better protected they are from the awkwardness that comes with self-negotiation. Attempting to negotiate one's own salary directly with a producer or general manager—the very individual you will soon report to—can be complicated. When negotiating on their own, an associate can be perceived as difficult or overly demanding while trying to fight for what they believe they are owed. An agent, on the other hand, possesses the necessary authority to engage in objective financial discussions, leaving the associate completely out of it. Furthermore, an agent can make sure their client is protected should contractual disputes or difficult situations arise during the contract. An agent is able to handle those situations on behalf of the associate allowing them to stay focused on the task at hand.

Associate contracts in regional theatre present a different challenge than securing work within the structured Broadway production. Most regional theatres lack a standardized "associate contract" overseen by SDC, meaning contract negotiations function on an "as needed" basis rather than adhering to established union minimums or shared industry terms. Because there are no set conditions or baseline expectations, the onus falls entirely upon the associate (or their representation) to meticulously analyse what is being offered. Therefore, it can be incredibly helpful to cross-reference any regional offer with the detailed provisions of a formal Broadway associate contract. Associate fees outside of Broadway are rarely comparable, and as a result, if a director or choreographer is set on hiring a specific associate, they may need to personally supplement the theatre's budget to secure them.

As a director and choreographer, I have made it a point to extend additional compensation to virtually every associate who has worked with me on a regional theatre production. I am aware of the amount of prep work that I expect my associate to put in before rehearsals start and I understand that most fees will not cover this period. My goal is to make sure that they never feel taken advantage of. I am especially grateful to those associates who feel confident enough to approach me and request assistance with their fee—a conversation that can be uncomfortable for anyone. By keeping the dialogue open and assisting whenever possible, I hope to create an environment where they feel seen, respected, and truly valued.

PART EIGHT
BECOMING YOUR OWN DIRECTOR AND/OR CHOREOGRAPHER

My Journey

After years spent refining my craft as an associate, the desire to step into the role of director and choreographer became undeniable. I had been incredibly fortunate to work alongside some of the industry's most brilliant creatives, absorbing every piece of information, every nuance of leadership, and every spark of artistic vision, preparing myself to one day steer the ship on my own. I was hungry to take all I had learned and lead the creative process myself, bringing my own distinct artistic vision to fruition. As I began this transition, I was constantly reminded of the wisdom Jeff Calhoun had used to lead every room I had been fortunate to be a part of: "*best idea wins*." This mantra became a guiding light, allowing me to relieve myself of the pressure of having to have all the answers and, instead, empowering me to create a collaborative and open room. This philosophy, plus the advice from many other mentors to surround myself with individuals I deeply respect and trust, allowed me to take the next steps in my career. I was aware that the industry knew me predominantly by the title "associate," so I would need to take the necessary steps to reinvent myself to ultimately be recognized as *the* director or *the* choreographer. Although I fully acknowledge there are many paths one can take on this journey, I will focus specifically on my own experiences.

The transition began with the decision to market myself exclusively as a choreographer. I started this by reaching out to creatives I had previously worked alongside, informing them of my aspirations to be a choreographer in my own right. The hope was that they would help introduce me to directors who might be looking for a choreographer. I was also hoping that should they ever be offered a job they were unable to accept because of scheduling conflicts, my name would be on the top of their list for referrals. Simultaneously, I began the process of updating all my professional materials—my resume, reel, and website—demonstrating my ability to be a true leader on my own. I then connected with my agent and explained my ambition to be seen less as the associate and more as the choreographer. The most significant part of this transition was the outreach: I contacted every theatre and industry contact I had made over the years, expressing my interest in being considered for any of their upcoming productions. The transition from associate to choreographer proved to be the toughest and lengthiest part of my entire career. I understood the hesitation; I had never choreographed a show on my own and many theatres perceived this as a lack of "choreographic experience." Yet, despite this apprehension, I kept pushing forward as I knew I was ready.

After what felt like an endless wait, the email that would change everything finally landed in my inbox: a message from the New Theatre in Kansas City, KS wanting to discuss a potential upcoming choreographic opportunity. The theatre was set to do a production of *All Shook Up*, and choreographer Lisa Stevens, who I had worked with previously on multiple projects, had graciously put my name forward since she was unavailable. The theatre flew me out for an interview with Richard Carrothers who was the artistic director of the theatre and would be directing *All Shook Up*. Once I arrived, Richard and I had a meeting where I pitched my creative concepts and ideas for the show's many musical numbers. I thought back to all the creatives I had previously been the associate to and how they would prepare presentations of their concepts and ideas for the team. Having this knowledge proved to be very fruitful. I was prepared with detailed mood boards outlining my vision, filmed sections of preliminary choreography, which I had previously developed and captured in New York City with a group of dancers, showcasing my stylistic approach, and a plethora of research. The meeting was a success; we forged an instant connection, and he was genuinely impressed by the thorough preparation and detailed nature of my presentation. Before I knew it, the contract was signed, solidifying my first professional choreography opportunity. It was because of my strong professional relationship with Lisa Stevens and being in the right place at the right time that would secure this opportunity.

The success of my professional theatre choreography debut came down to two things I pride myself on: preparation and organization. I approached the process with everything carefully mapped out and planned, which allowed me to walk into the room with a clear vision while staying flexible and adaptable. Every process comes with curve balls—a piece of choreography simply doesn't translate to the performers as hoped, the inevitable moment when a prop arrives and fails to function as you had planned, a dancer isn't able to make their entrance because they need more time for a costume change . . . the list goes on. Yet, because I had that detailed structure in place, when these challenges arose, I could adapt immediately, finding a solution in the moment, and just as quickly get myself back on track, preventing my entire prep from unravelling.

Ultimately, this process became a huge lesson, not just in my skills as a choreographer, but most importantly, in the art of collaboration. Stepping into a rehearsal room with a director I had never worked with before was nerve-wracking. Yet, beneath the initial nerves and jitters, I stayed calm and took all that previous experience and knowledge I had learned and applied it. One of the biggest things I took away from this experience was the importance of communication, not just with the director, but across the entire creative team. I needed to be articulate, clear, and precise when presenting my ideas and concepts to ensure they were perfectly understood. Making sure the costume designer knew exactly what a dancer would be doing in a specific costume to allow the movement I needed. Making sure a prop was just the right size and weight that it could be tossed from one actor to another. Making sure a dancer's wig wasn't too long and wouldn't get in the way of her partner. This constant communication is what allows for a successful collaboration. I took all the lessons I had learned on *All Shook Up* and applied them to every process I had moving forward.

I would go on to continue working at the New Theatre choreographing *The Sound of Music, Joseph and the Amazing Technicolor Dreamcoat, Pump Boys and Dinettes, Hairspray, Forever Plaid, Chicago* and then was offered the opportunity to direct *and* choreograph *Smokey Joe's Café.*

The Sound of Music proved to be an unprecedented experience. When I was initially asked to choreograph the show, I explained that my availability was limited to only the first week and a half of rehearsals—an inconvenience I anticipated would lead them to seeking another choreographer. To my surprise, the team was eager to work with me on this production and came up with a plan: I would come in and choreograph every single musical number within the first few days, then

Todd DuBail in *All Shook Up* at the New Theatre.

Credit: New Theatre

Ron Bohmer and Leigh Ann Larkin in *The Sound of Music* at the New Theatre.

Credit: New Theatre

depart, leaving the director to stage the rest of the show. This unusual arrangement demanded a serious amount of preparation. Weeks leading up to the first rehearsal, the director and I engaged in extensive creative meetings, planning every detail: the exact placement of every piece of furniture to make sure I was using the space correctly, where each prop would be preset, exact entrances for each cast member. Every possible question that could be asked, was! My work would largely be set in stone before any scene work began so this knowledge was crucial to make sure the director and I were completely aligned. The performers were quite overwhelmed by the sheer amount of movement they were learning upfront, especially since they had barely even learned the music. Yet, thanks to the meticulous amount of preparation that had been done, the plan succeeded, reminding me again of the importance of preparation and organization.

By the time I got asked to choreograph *Hairspray*, my fifth production at the New Theatre, I felt that I had earned the right to ask if I could bring on an Associate Choreographer, as I would need the assistance to get the job done. Because of the fast-paced nature of the rehearsal process and the way this particular show is structured, it was imperative to have multiple rooms running at the same time, which made having an associate so important. I turned to my trusted colleague, Andrew Turteltaub, whom I had previously worked with as a performer. Although Andrew had a long list of credits in the commercial and television world, he was looking to expand his skills as a theatre choreographer. Having dedicated years to mastering the craft of being an associate, I now needed to understand how to utilize this position for myself. Andrew and I's approach to *Hairspray* was carefully planned, starting with extensive choreography pre-pro in New York City, where a group of dancers helped us block out several of the many dances. We then moved on to documenting every piece of blocking and every transition into a shared master document, guaranteeing we would be completely aligned, even if we were working in separate spaces. As we began the rehearsal period, I quickly learned the profound trust required to delegate one's work to an associate, confident that they would teach it with precision and nuance in your absence. I knew Andrew possessed the keen eye and dedication to perfectly translate every detail we had discussed onto the company. When the *Kansas City Star* noted, ". . . special recognition goes to Richard J. Hinds for the exceptional choreography," my first thought was of Andrew, for without his partnership, such recognition would simply not have been possible.

Christopher Brasfield in *Hairspray* at the New Theatre.

Credit: New Theatre

After a collection of successful productions at the New Theatre, I was honored to be asked to step into the role of director *AND* choreographer for *Smokey Joes Café.* This show's lack of script leaves no real blueprint for how to weave a narrative together, allowing for complete creative freedom, enabling me to infuse the production with my own artistic vision. With Andrew once again by my side as my associate, we started the journey. While striving to make sure my choreography is always rooted in narrative, applying that to an entire production with forty songs and no script was an ambitious undertaking. The process began by diving into the brilliant songwriting of Leiber and Stoller and understanding the theatricality and storytelling within their lyrics. I then turned my attention to the song order, attempting to understand the intended progression and the story that could be uncovered. Collaborating with the design team, we meticulously crafted the world of the show, establishing the distinct "neighborhood" setting for Act 1 and the iconic "Smokey Joe's Café" for Act 2. When we commenced rehearsals with the cast, featuring standout talents such as Melody Betts, James T. Lane, and Alexander Aguilar, we started by discussing each of the characters and their stories. Making this be the first thing we tackled, stressed how important approaching the material from an acting perspective was to me. I viewed this show much more than a jukebox musical. The critical reception showed that all of our hard work had paid off. The *Kansas City Star* wrote "Director/choreographer Richard J. Hinds has assembled a superior cast and manages to do something remarkable: A show without dialogue or spoken commentary that finds a glimmer of transcendent meaning. This is more than a collection of pop tunes. The show is ultimately about the power of music."

Having now successfully broken into the professional world as a "choreographer," I was armed with a collection of reviews, production photos, and video content to begin reaching out to even

Melody A. Betts in *Smokey Joe's Café* at the New Theatre.

Credit: New Theatre

more theatres and creatives. This time, however, requests for meetings were being taken more seriously. I felt confident in how I was able to promote myself, with a body of work behind me, and I was also now in a place to start exploring flexing my directorial skills and presenting myself as such. The range of shows I had previously worked on made me highly enticing to theatres who quickly recognized my versatility and how my skills could serve several of their potential upcoming shows as they were settling on their seasons.

My history working on the original Broadway productions of *Newsies* and *Come From Away* proved to be a huge advantage when these titles became available for regional licensing. Regional theatres are more frequently seeking out individuals who have previously served as an associate on the original run of a show, as they possess deep knowledge regarding that specific production. These associates often come equipped with vital resources including relationships with alumni, which offers huge benefits, especially because of the quick rehearsal processes. For these regional theatres, knowing the person leading the charge has deep rooted knowledge of the show makes them incredibly enticing.

When I was approached regarding *Newsies* and *Come From Away*, the question was often the same: *Would I prefer to stage a recreation of the original version, or use my knowledge of the*

Joey Barreiro and Danny Quadrino in *Newsies* at Pittsburgh CLO.
Credit: Matt Polk

material to create something entirely new? For me, the choice was easy—although knowing a show inside and out provides a deep sense of comfort, I find a much greater artistic challenge in starting fresh, which also allows me to put my own stamp on the show. This approach was only heightened by the fact that I was still carving out my identity as a director and choreographer. Replicating someone else's vision felt like I would be stifling the very growth I was eager to find.

While directing and choreographing *Newsies* at Pittsburgh CLO, I faced an incredibly tight ten-day rehearsal process, which prompted me to hire several alumni from Broadway and the national tour. With the permission of original Broadway Director Jeff Calhoun, I was able to incorporate some of his direction to help with this expedited schedule. We utilized a rental set that was distinctly different from the original Broadway design, requiring that much of the blocking be reconceived. Although I had been involved with the show from its early stages on the directorial side, the choreography was not part of my DNA. This freedom allowed me to develop an entirely new choreographic language, unbound by any preconceived steps or musical accents. I surrounded myself with an incredible associate, Phil Colgan, whose fresh perspective—coming with no prior knowledge of the show—brought many new ideas to the production. Having the opportunity to create my own definitive version made me a valuable resource, and I was subsequently invited to direct and choreograph the show at La Mirada Theatre and 5 Star Theatricals.

Wes Williams and Company in *Newsies* at 5 Star Theatricals.
Credit: Jeff Ditto Photography

Rema Webb, Erica Spyres, Andréa Burns, and Lisa Helmi Johanson in *Come From Away* at Paper Mill Playhouse.

Credit: Jeremy Daniel

Richard J. Hinds and Elyn Collier in rehearsals for *Tootsie* at North Shore Music Theatre.

Credit: Fred Sullivan

Richard J. Hinds and Marjorie Failoni in rehearsals for *La Cage aux Folles* at The Muny.

Credit: The Muny

Taking on the role of director and choreographer for *Come From Away* at Ogunquit Playhouse, I challenged myself to completely reinvent the show without holding onto any of Christopher Ashley's original direction or Kelly Devine's choreography. I came up with an actor-musician concept with the rule that the actors would never play an instrument as their character, but only as an extension of another character's emotional state. This concept meant many of the alumni I had previously worked with were not a fit for this iteration. I deliberately assembled a team without intimate knowledge of the original Broadway staging, including our incredible Music Director, Sam Groisser, and my brilliant Associate Director and Choreographer, Elyn Collier. I would get a nice chuckle when someone on the team would suggest an idea, and my immediate response would be, *"We already did that. Try again."* I was adamant that we build our *new* version of the show.

After many years in this business, I have struck a balance that allows me to divide my time between being an associate and taking on my own creative projects. Getting to this place required a lot of learning and patience. As my career path continues to evolve, I am still drawn to associate work. I love being able to absorb new perspectives, expand my network, and collaborate with creatives who inspire me. I've always embraced the mantra, *"I don't have all the answers,"* and working alongside creatives in an associate capacity sharpens my craft and makes me be a better director and choreographer.

Now that I am in a place where I can hire Associate Directors and Choreographers to join my team, I constantly reflect on all the lessons learned from my own journey and bring that knowledge

Lizz Picini and Richard J. Hinds in rehearsal for *Guys and Dolls* at The Finger Lakes Musical Theatre Festival.

Credit: The Finger Lakes Musical Theatre Festival

with me. I seek collaborators who embody the same dedication and passion I have. Having once stood where my associates now stand, I am acutely aware of the importance of empowerment. I encourage their voices in rehearsals and decision making, creating space for their creativity to flourish. When their suggestions shape a production, I make sure their contributions are known to the room, ensuring recognition. I push to make sure their name appears on any title page that mine is on. I want any associate I work with to know how much I value them on my team. Many of them aspire to become directors and choreographers themselves, and I make it a priority to support them just as so many supported me. I strive to foster an environment where every collaborator feels valued, heard, and inspired to reach their full potential.

Your Journey

The path of a freelance director or choreographer is rarely the same and will be filled with exhilarating highs and challenging lows. One year your calendar will be booked solid only for the next to be incredibly sparse. This unpredictability requires you to never get complacent, regardless of where you are in your career. The work never truly stops. Continuously reaching out to theatres and cultivating new relationships with artistic directors is essential, always hopeful that these connections will turn into possible opportunities down the line. It is imperative to always have a handful of dream shows in your back pocket—productions that genuinely intrigue you, for which you've already sketched out some initial conceptual approaches. Whether a regional theatre approaches you with a specific show they envision you directing or choreographing, or they ask you to propose a project of your own, being ready with well-considered ideas can make all the difference.

Look around for writers who are creating new material. Introduce yourself to these creatives, attend their readings, engage with their work, and build genuine relationships. You never know when a fellow writer's project will secure funding, and they'll need a trusted creative to bring their vision to life. By fostering these connections early, you position yourself to potentially be on their team.

Let your own ideas marinate. What untold stories stir your imagination? A quirky character, a historical event begging for reimagining, or a fresh take on a classic theme—these ideas could grow into a compelling play or musical. When you envision these projects, think about who you would like to collaborate with on them.

Success in this field isn't just about talent—it's about the opportunities you make for yourself through proactive creativity and collaboration. The journey will certainly have challenges, rejections, and periods of uncertainty; however, the ultimate reward is witnessing your show reach its opening night, seeing your vision materialize on stage. It makes every single up and down worth it.

PART NINE
IN CONCLUSION

The journey to becoming an Associate Director or Associate Choreographer is deeply personal and unique, shaped by your connections, timing, and, above all, patience. There is no single roadmap to success. With an average of 30–45 Broadway shows opening each year, opportunities at the highest level are limited. Patience and persistence are essential, whether you are just starting out or already have a string of successful contracts.

Broadway is only one part of the picture. Tours, regional theatres, cruise lines, and even theme parks can offer experiences that are equally rewarding and creatively enriching. Every opportunity, whether it unfolds as planned or takes unforeseen turns, provides lessons, growth, and insights that will shape your craft. The theatre community is remarkably tight-knit, and your professional reputation travels ahead of you. Leading with grace, professionalism, and kindness is paramount—momentary lapses in judgment or integrity can have long-lasting consequences. Treating everyone with respect and maintaining integrity will carry you further than talent alone.

Associates are often the unsung heroes of theatre. They are a versatile creative force, sometimes leading a room from the front with authority, other times quietly observing from the back and absorbing every detail. Typically, they are the first to arrive and the last to leave, juggling multiple responsibilities while maintaining calm, steady energy throughout the production. High-pressure situations, strong personalities, and rapid-fire decision-making are the norm, and navigating them with poise is essential. Through it all, two qualities remain indispensable: unwavering preparation and impeccable organization.

Becoming an Associate Director or Choreographer is not merely a career choice—it is a professional and personal commitment. The path demands passion, perseverance, and a deep dedication to your craft. Long hours, complex problemsolving, and challenges that test your patience and resilience are inevitable. Yet, amidst the intensity, it is essential to be kind to yourself. Celebrate small victories, learn from setbacks, and embrace the lessons that arise from unexpected challenges.

Surround yourself with mentors, collaborators, and peers who inspire you. Stay curious, stay humble, and remain open to new ideas. Every rehearsal, performance, and interaction is an opportunity to sharpen your skills, expand your perspective, and strengthen your voice. Trust your instincts, but also remain adaptable—sometimes compromise and seeing the bigger picture are the keys to success.

Ultimately, your journey is uniquely yours, and your contributions are invaluable. The goals and dreams you hold, when paired with dedication, effort, and patience, are achievable. Embrace the process, trust yourself, and approach every opportunity with energy, focus, and professionalism. You are capable of more than you realize, and the theatre world will be richer for the creativity, insight, and passion you bring. Go get 'em.

Richard J. Hinds at the age of 9.

Credit: Angela D'Valda Sirico and Steve Sirico

GLOSSARY

BLOCKING: The precise staging of the actors and their path of movement in scenes. The term "blocking" came into popular use in the 1960s based on the tradition of nineteenth-century theatre directors who worked out their scenes on a mini model of the stage, using blocks to represent actors.

BLOCKING BIBLE: A comprehensive and detailed document to record all the movement and action in a theatrical production. It serves as the definitive record of the show's staging.

CALL BOARD: A noticeboard backstage in the theatre where actor's typically sign-in. Other information you might find on this board include Actor's Equity Association (AEA) rules, dressing room assignments, who is performing in that day's performance, and several calendars including monthly schedules as well as call times for the next rehearsal or performance.

CONTINGENCY: An alternative plan of action if a piece of technology fails to operate. It is vital that contingencies are worked out in advance so that as soon as something goes wrong, the show can continue safely, and the audience will hopefully be unaware.

CUT SHOW: A performance (usually of a musical) that doesn't have the required number of cast available to run the entire show with all choreography and characters on stage. Some elements are cut to ensure that the performance goes ahead with the minimum amount of disruption visible to the audience, even though the cast on stage may be smaller than usual.

DANCE CAPTAIN: A person who is responsible for maintaining the show's choreography and artistic quality after the choreographer leaves. They will lead the company in choreography rehearsals and will regularly work with understudies, swings, and replacement company members to ensure they are ready to hit the stage. Dance captains usually know the movement and choreography for every character in a show. They typically are a swing or an ensemble member.

DRY TECH: A technical rehearsal held *without the actors*, focusing solely on integrating and timing the production's technical elements such as lighting, sound cues, scene changes, and special effects, allowing the crew to perfect their operations before performers are involved.

FROZEN: Means the production has reached a point (usually near opening or after previews) where creative changes stop, and all elements—acting, lighting, sound, sets, costumes—are locked in for the official opening night, with the creative team generally stepping back.

GOD MIC: A microphone, usually in the front of house or backstage, used by the stage manager or creative team to communicate with the cast and crew on stage or in dressing rooms without the audience hearing.

GROUND PLAN: A scaled plan (overhead) view of the theatre stage area or of a set design. The ground plan shows all items standing on the stage floor and any permanent items that will affect the production, and the position of any flown pieces.

HALF-HOUR: The 30 minutes before actors are required to be on stage and ready to begin. Performers are expected to be in the building preparing for performance, including warming up, and getting into costume, hair, and makeup.

I.A.T.S.E.: *International Alliance of Theatrical Stage Employees*; Stage employees union.

INVITED CALL: An audition session where only specific actors, typically submitted by their agents or selected by the casting director based on their headshot and resume, are asked to attend at a scheduled time.

OFF-BOOK: An actor or cast who has memorized their lines no longer requiring the use of a script.

OPEN CALL: A casting call where any actor, regardless of experience or agent, can show up to audition.

OPENING NIGHT: Typically after a preview period, this performance is the production as it will be performed from here on out. Reviews for productions are published only after the curtain goes up on this performance.

PANTOMIME: A type of British family-friendly interactive theatrical comedy based on a fairy tale, featuring exaggerated characters, audience participation, and broad humor for all ages.

PAPER TECH: A session without the set or actors when the stage management team, creative team, and designers talk through the show ensuring everything is clearly mapped out and documented appropriately. The director and choreographer will be instrumental to this session as this is when they make sure their vision is aligned with the entire team. They will clearly articulate where they see specific cues happening allowing everyone to update their paperwork and to help prepare for the technical process.

PER DIEM: A daily payment by an employer to cover daily living expenses. This is in addition to a fee.

PRE-PRODUCTION: Planning phase of production before actors rehearse (or sometimes have even been cast). Brings together the production team in discussions about style, possibilities, and budgets.

PREVIEWS: The first performances of a show. Previews indicate that the show is in flux. The creative team may make changes to the show night to night. During this time, the company performs by night and rehearses by day.

PROSCENIUM STAGE: A common orientation of a theatre. The stage is framed like a picture by the proscenium arch, with the stage on one side opposite the audience.

PUT-IN REHEARSAL: An on-stage run-through for a new cast member, understudy, or swing to integrate their role into the production with full technical elements (sets, costumes, lights) and the rest of the company, usually guided by the stage manager and dance captain.

REPLICA PRODUCTION: A production that closely copies the original Broadway or West End direction, choreography, and technical elements to recreate the production in new venues and on tour.

RESIDENT CHOREOGRAPHER: A person hired to maintain the quality and consistency of a show's dance elements over its entire run, handling cast changes, training swings/understudies, giving notes, and ensuring the original choreography's vision stays intact, essentially acting as the ongoing artistic guardian for the movement in the show.

RESIDENT DIRECTOR: A person hired to be the primary creative and logistical point person *after* opening night, ensuring the show's long-term quality by running understudy rehearsals, giving notes to the cast and crew, managing cast changes, and maintaining the original creative vision, essentially serving as the director's eyes and ears for the entire run.

ROLL OUT: Launching or opening the next company of an existing show, putting up the established production with a new cast and crew in a new location.

SDC: The *Stage Directors and Choreographers Society*, a US labor union that represents and protects the rights, health, and livelihoods of professional stage directors and choreographers, negotiating contracts for major productions (such as Broadway, Off-Broadway, and regional theatres). SDC advocates for fair pay, safe workplaces, and artistic rights, ensuring members have support and that the industry maintains high creative standards.

SHADOWING: An aspiring theatre professional (e.g., director, choreographer, stage manager) follows and observes an experienced professional to learn their techniques and the production process.

SITZPROBE: A rehearsal where the performers sing with the orchestra for the first time, focusing attention on integrating the two groups with no blocking or staging.

STAGE WRITE: A professional digital tool for theatre, used by directors, choreographers, dance captains, and stage managers to document and share all aspects of a show's staging, blocking, and cues in one place, allowing teams to track performer/scenery movement, annotate scripts, and create calling scripts efficiently. It's an industry standard, popular on Broadway, and also used as an online teaching resource for theatre arts.

STANDBY: A performer who knows all of the material for a lead role—and goes on if the principal actor is out—but does not otherwise perform in the show.

SWING: A performer who learns multiple ensemble roles (tracks) in a production, stepping in to cover for absent cast members because of illness, injury or vacation, ensuring the show can go on seamlessly. While understudies cover principal roles, swings cover the chorus/ensemble.

TECHNICAL REHEARSAL (TECH): The first time the show is rehearsed in the venue incorporating all technical elements including lighting, scenery, costumes, wigs, and sound as well as automation, pyro, projections, etc.

THRUST STAGE: A stage "thrust" into the audience, with the audience on three sides. Productions presented on these thrust stages are blocked with the three-sided audience in mind, so that you don't miss any action.

UNDERSTUDY: A performer cast in the ensemble of a musical (or minor role in a play) who is responsible for covering a lead and/or supporting role(s).

VACATION SWING: a performer who covers multiple ensemble or swing tracks for actors who are going on vacation or taking time off.

WANDELPROBE: A rehearsal where the performers and the orchestra run through a show, allowing performers to move and practice their staging and blocking while singing with the live music, with no focus on any other technical elements.

WING: The offstage area located to the left and right sides of the stage, hidden from the audience, where actors wait for entrances, props and set pieces are stored, and crew members prepare and coordinate cues.

WORK LIST: A *"to-do" list* or a *"punch list"* compiled by stage management and the creative team. This list will often include the page number in question, the scene and/or song, the actors involved, what the change is, and a cue line to ensure everyone begins precisely at the right place.

Resources

Hairspray
https://www.kansascity.com/entertainment/performing-arts/article21095178.html
Smokey Joe's Café
https://www.kansascity.com/entertainment/performing-arts/article634061.html

Associate Contributors

Ashley Andrews
Photo credit: Ross Ferguson

Ashley Rodbro
Photo credit: Michelle Grace Hunder © Global Creatures producer of Moulin Rouge! The Musical

Cedric Dodd
Photo credit: Lee Gumbs

Conner Wilson
Photo credit: Andy Henderson

DB Bonds
Photo credit: Pretty Woman: The Musical *UK*

Danny Sharron
Photo credit: Gene Reed Photography

Kasey RT Graham
Photo credit: Lauren Eliot Photography

Lauren Stroud
Photo credit: Alex Powell ©

Lizz Picini
Photo credit: Jon Taylor

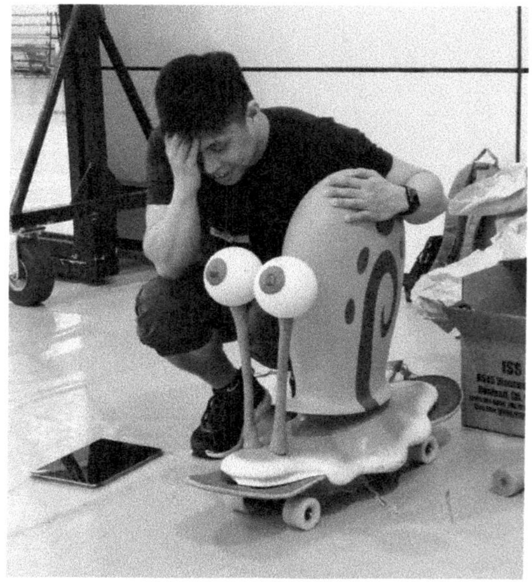

Lou Castro
Photo credit: Lou Castro

Rachelle Rak
Photo credit: Andrew Holtz

Rickey Tripp
Photo credit: Trey Thomas

Sarah Parker
Photo credit: Stephanie Crousillat

Tavia Rivée Jefferson
Photo credit: Ambe J. Williams

Travis Waldschmidt
Photo credit: Angela Marie Orellana

Voltaire Wade-Green
Photo credit: Bruce Glikas

INDEX